By special arrangement with

New Shoes Theatre in associ
Finborough Theatre presents

The first UK production in

JEANNIE

by Aimée Stuart

FINBOROUGH | THEATRE
VIBRANT **NEW WRITING** | UNIQUE **REDISCOVERIES**

First performed at the Torch Theatre, London: Tuesday, 6 February 1940.
Transferred to the Wyndham's Theatre, London: Wednesday, 3 April 1940.
First performed at the Finborough Theatre: Tuesday, 27 November 2018.

JEANNIE

by Aimée Stuart

Cast in order of speaking

Father	**Kim Durham**
Jeannie	**Mairi Hawthorn**
Mrs. Whitelaw	**Madeleine Hutchins**
Bessie	**Carol Holt**
Maggie	**Evelyn Adams**
Stanley Smith	**Matthew Mellalieu**
Porter	**Max Alexander-Taylor**
Attendant	**Max Alexander-Taylor**
Reception Clerk	**Kim Durham**
The Blonde	**Madeleine Hutchins**
The Count	**Patrick Pearson**
Hotel Waiter	**Max Alexander-Taylor**
Page	**Max Alexander-Taylor**
Smaller Page	**Max Alexander-Taylor**
An American	**Evelyn Adams**
Waiter	**Kim Durham**
The Mistress	**Carol Holt**
Her Husband	**Kim Durham**

The action takes place in 1936 in a little country town in Scotland, Vienna and Glasgow.

The performance lasts approximately two hours.

There will be one interval of fifteen minutes.

Director	**Nicolette Kay**
Set and Costume Design	**James Helps**
Lighting Designer	**Holly Ellis**
Sound Designer	**Rachael Murray**
Stage Manager	**Ann Bailey**
Assistant Director	**Millie Foy**
Production Manager	**Pamela Schermann**

Our patrons are respectfully reminded that, in this intimate theatre, any noise such as rustling programmes, talking or the ringing of mobile phones may distract the actors and your fellow audience-members.

We regret there is no admittance or re-admittance to the auditorium whilst the performance is in progress.

Evelyn Adams | Maggie/The American Woman
Trained at Italia Conti.
Theatre includes *Horrible Histories* (National Tour),
Where The Wild Things Are (Unicorn Theatre, *The
Ringer* (Gaiety Theatre), *Mother Goose* (The Theatre,
Chipping Norton), *Institute of Impossibility* (Belgrade
Theatre, Coventry), *My Name is Hunger* (Park
Theatre), *Father of the Bride* (The Mill at Sonning),
The Ghost Train (Brockley Jack Studio Theatre), *Dry
Rot* (National Tour) and *Count Oederland* (Arcola
Theatre).
Film includes *Gravity, Meet Me on the Southbank,
Deadinburgh* and *The Secret Life of Butterflies.*
Television includes *Seven and Me* and *Doctors.*

Max Alexander-Taylor | Waiter/Porter/Ensemble
Trained at the Royal Conservatoire of Scotland.
Theatre while training includes *London Road* (Royal
Conservatoire of Scotland), *Spring Awakening* (Dundee
Repertory Theatre) and *Side Show* (West Brewery).

Kim Durham | Father/Clerk/Herr Ober
Theatre includes *The Faith Healer* (Gate Theatre,
Dublin), *The Lady from the Sea* and *Beauty and the
Beast* (Birmingham Rep), *A Christmas Carol* (Library
Theatre, Manchester), *Sitting Pretty* (Theatre of
Comedy, *The Wind in the Willows, Othello, Our
Country's Good, The Rivals* and *Man of the Moment*
(Swan Theatre, Worcester).
Film includes *Mike Bassett: England Manager*
Television includes *Inspector Morse, The Tenant of
Wildfell Hall* and *New Tricks.*
Radio includes over one hundred radio dramas,
including twenty years in *The Archers.*
Kim recently completed a long full-time position as a
Senior Acting Tutor and Course Leader for the MA in
Professional Acting at Bristol Old Vic Theatre School.

Mairi Hawthorn | Jeannie
Trained at Guildhall School of Music and Drama.
Theatre includes *Macbeth* (Stafford Festival
Shakespeare) and *Wishbone* (The Bunker).
Theatre while training includes *Balm in Gilead, As You
Like It, The Same Deep Water As Me, Crazy For You,
How To Succeed In Business Without Really Trying,
The Merchant of Venice, Medea* and *Uncle Vanya.*
Television includes *Game of Thrones.*
Radio includes *Sea Longing.*

Carol Holt | Bessie/Mistress
Trained at Welsh College of Music and Drama.
Theatre includes *Billy Liar* (Ashcroft Theatre, Croydon), *Great Pretenders* (New End Theatre, Hampstead), *How The Other Half Loves* (Coliseum Theatre, Oldham), *The Shell Seekers* (Nick Brooke Productions), *Mixed Feelings* (TEG Productions), *What The Butler Saw* and *Two* (Dukes Playhouse, Lancaster), *Norman Conquests* (Harrogate Theatre), *Blithe Spirit* (Harrogate Theatre) and *The Resistible Rise of Arturo Ui* (Library Theatre, Manchester).
Film includes *The Bris* and *Small Time Revolutionary*.
Television includes *Doctors, Emmerdale, Coronation Street, Pearly Gates, The Royal Today, The Royal, Is Harry on the Boat, Surprising Stars, Baddiel's Syndrome* and *Bob Martin*.

Madeleine Hutchins | Mrs.Whitelaw/The Blonde
Trained at East 15 Acting School.
Theatre includes *Mrs.Warren's Profession* (McCarter Theatre, Princeton), *Hay Fever, As You Like It* and *You Never Can Tell* (National Tour), *Stone Cold Murder, Reasons to Be Pretty, Boeing Boeing, Don't Misunderstand Me* and *Don't Lose the Place* (English Theatre, Hamburg), *Unnatural Tragedy* which was nominated for an OffWestEnd Award (White Bear Theatre), *Before I Sleep* which won the Peter Brook Award (dreamthinkspeak), *Macbeth* and *A Midsummer Night's Dream* (TourdeForce), *Shaw's Women* (Jane Nightwork Productions) and *Confessions Off Broadway* (Grand Theatre, Swansea).
Film includes *Nasty*, which premiered at the BFI London Film Festival and for which Madeleine won the Award of Merit at The IndieFEST Film Awards and Best Actress at Fly Film Festival.
Television includes *Fright Bites, Thanks For the Memories* and *Candice Renoir.*

Matthew Mellalieu | Stanley Smith
Trained at Drama Centre, London.
Theatre includes *After the Dance* (Theatre by the Lake, Keswick), *As You Like It* (Shared Experience and Theatre by the Lake, Keswick), *Henry V* and *Macbeth* (Globe Education), *Julius Caesar, As You Like It, A Midsummer Night's Dream, The Wind in the Willows, Romeo and Juliet* and *The Nativity* (Iris Theatre) and *The Tempest* (Rosemary Branch Theatre).
Film includes *Remora, Dark Show, The Rise of the Krays, The Brother* and *Made of Honour.*
Television includes *Casualty, Love, Lies and Records, Still Open All Hours, Doctors, Rovers* and *Hollyoaks.*

Patrick Pearson | The Count

Trained at the Central School of Speech and Drama.
Theatre includes *The Madness of George III*
(National Theatre), *When We Are Married* (Whitehall
Theatre), *A Piece of My Mind* (Apollo Theatre), *Great
Balls of Fire* (Cambridge Theatre), *The Mousetrap* (St
Martin's Theatre), *Eastern Star* (Tara Arts Theatre), *A
Perfect Retreat* (Bush Theatre), *Take a Chance on Me*
(New End Theatre, Hampstead), *An Inspector Calls*
and *Mary Rose* (Greenwich Theatre), *Point Valaine*
(Chichester Festival Theatre), *The Duchess of Malfi*
and *Time and the Conways* (Bristol Old Vic), *What
the Butler Saw* (Royal Lyceum Theatre, Edinburgh),
The School for Wives and *Tom Jones* (Leeds
Playhouse) and *The Writing Game* (Birmingham
Rep).

Film includes *The Best Exotic Marigold Hotel*, *The
Nutcracker* and *Privates on Parade*.

Television includes *The Government Inspector*,
Closing Numbers, *EastEnders*, *New Tricks*, *Hostages*,
A Dangerous Man, *Bad Girls*, *Casualty*, *The Bill*,
Lovejoy, *Poldark*, *Too Good to be True*, *The Worst
Witch*, *When We Are Married*, *Dangerfield*, *Goodnight
Sweetheart*, *Pie in the Sky*, *Hetty Wainthrop
Investigates*, *Brass*, *Nice Work*, *The Contractor*,
Frederick Forsyth Presents, *Vote for Them*, *The
Death of the Heart* and *We'll Meet Again*.

Aimée Stuart | Playwright

Amy Constance McHardy was born in 1886 in Glasgow, to Mercy McHardy, a Milliner and William McHardy, a Wine Merchant. She changed her name to Aimée while living in Paris with her lover, William "Bill" Bond, an English journalist. Bill was awarded the Military Cross and Bar for bravery, they married in London in 1917. He returned to France as a fighter pilot, seven months later he was shot down and killed. Aimée published their passionate and intimate war correspondence soon after his death as *An Airman's Wife* under the name of Aimée McHardy.

She then published *A Pair of Vagabonds* (1919) under the name Aimée Bond. The novel follows two women who dispense coffee and cigarettes to allied troops near the French Front, for the 'Comité Anglais', a women's unit of the 'Oeuvre de Jus'. In her next novel, *Mona Lisa Nobody* (1920), she portrays a young, naïve, female Scottish journalist in pre-WWI Bohemian Paris.

In 1924, Aimée married Philip Stuart and the couple became well known for co-writing successful plays and entertaining artists, writers and actors in their Carlton House Terrace salon. A favourite greeting between the bisexual (or "ambisextrous" as Aimée called it) group was "Hello darling, how's your sex life?".

Aimée and Philip Stuart poached their personal lives to use as characters and settings in their plays – *The Cat's Cradle* (1929) is about the London theatre scene. *Her Shop* (1929) and *Sixteen* (1934) are set in millinery and dressmaking businesses and it seems no coincidence that Aimée's mother was the proprietor of the renowned Mercie Mchardy millinery establishments in central London and Manchester. *Nine till Six* (1930) is also set in a fashionable clothes salon, and during the long run it drew press attention and a lesbian following for its all-female cast. *Supply and Demand* (1931) is set in the colonial British Raj in India where Philip Stuart was born.

Love of Women (1934) was banned by the Lord Chamberlain and despite Aimée's pleas and offers to revise the lesbian theme the Duchess Theatre production was cancelled. Shortly afterwards, Aimée and Philip Stuart set sail for the opening of their play *Birthday* (1934) at the 49th Street Theater, New York

Philip died in 1936, aged 48, from alcoholism and Aimée left London to stay with friends in Vienna. By this time their plays were produced all over the world, in the West End, the regions, adapted for the screen and were a staple for amateur and professional companies.

Jeannie was the first play Aimée Stuart wrote without Philip and despite the resistance by producers to its many scene changes, it opened in February 1940 in the Off-West End Torch Theatre directed by Irene Hentschel. The newcomer Barbara Mullen achieved overnight stardom in the title role and it transferred to the Wyndham's Theatre, however by mid-September the Blitz had caused the theatre to close along with virtually all the theatres in the West End.

Jeannie transferred to Broadway, was also broadcast by BBC radio and Anatole de Grunwald and Roland Pertwee adapted the play for a film version (1941) starring Barbara Mullen and Michael Redgrave. It was later rewritten and filmed as a musical set in contemporary USA and released as *Let's Be Happy* (1954).

During the war Aimée Stuart wrote additional dialogue for successful films including *The Gentle Sex* (1943), *Fanny by Gaslight* (1944) and *The Wicked Lady* (1946) and she later wrote the film adaptation of *The Golden Madonna* (1949).

Among her post-war plays are *Lace on Her Petticoat* (1950), later adapted for Film and TV, *A Gentleman's Daughter* (1953) which escaped the censor despite a lesbian character, *Where the Heart Is* (1955) and *A Breath of Scandal* (1958). In 1954 the BBC broadcast *Jeannie* live on BBC TV and in 1957 *Fair Passenger* was the first play to be broadcast live on ABC TV in Melbourne, Australia.

Well into old age, Aimée Stuart was fondly regarded for encouraging young writers, dining with them at The Ivy. She died in 1981 at the age of 95 in Brighton. Her posthumous film credit is for additional dialogue in Michael Winner's remake of *The Wicked Lady* (1983).

Nicolette Kay | Director

Productions at the Finborough Theatre include the world premiere of *Seed*, *Love Child* and *Hurried Steps*.

Trained at Drama Centre, London. Theatre as director includes Time Out Critics' Choice production of *Mary Stuart*, *The Dreams of Clytemnestra and Mela* all by Dacia Maraini (BAC), *My Name Is Antonino Calderone* (MAC), *The B3 Team* (Lyric Studio, Hammersmith) and the British premiere of *Mud* (Etcetera Theatre). Nicolette founded Muzikansky and New Shoes Theatre companies.

Writing includes the co-translations of *Mary Stuart* and *My Name Is Antonino Calderone* both of which are published. She contributed a Chapter to *Il Sogno Del Teatro: Cronaca Di Una Passione* about Dacia Maraini. Her full-length play *Falling Out* won an Arts Council Award.

Her screenplay, *A Short Message*, was filmed at the Rutger Hauer Filmfactory. Her TEDx talk is called *Hidden Stories, Hurried Steps* (TEDx CoventGardenWomen).

As a professional actress, Nicolette played leads with many companies including Cambridge Theatre Company, Derby Playhouse, the Gate Theatre, The Women's Theatre Group and The Young Vic.

James Helps | Set and Costume Designer
Trained at Eastbourne and Wimbledon School of Art.
Theatre with Nicolette Kay includes *Mary Stuart* (BAC) and *My
Name is Antonino Calderone* (MAC).
Theatre includes *1599* (Stackpool Playhouse, Bristol), *Foreign
Field*, *After the Fall*, *The Plough and the Stars*, *Spokesong*, *The
Comedians* and *A Christmas Carol* (Lyric Theatre, Belfast), *A
Small Family Business* (Northcott Theatre, Exeter), *Shakespeare*
(The Tobacco Factory, Bristol) and *Walking the Chains* (Brunel's
Passenger Shed).
Film includes *Leon the Pig Farmer, Beyond Bedlam, On Dangerous
Ground* and *Midnight Man*.
Dance includes Janet Smith and Dancers Enchanted Places, and
Wayne Sleep's Dash.
James Helps has been Head of Design at the Arts Theatre Ipswich,
the Nuffield Southampton Theatre, the Renaissance Theatre in
Cumbria and the Marlowe Theatre, Canterbury.
Having taken eleven years out to teach, James returned to Design
work to Production Design the Community Feature Film *The
Happylands* for Theatre Workshop Scotland, and The Hatching. He
has produced for Fat Chance with productions at Bristol Old Vic
and for Theatre Royal Bath, for whom he produced and co-wrote
Monument directed by Patrick Robinson for HTV.
He is currently an Associate Lecturer in Production Design at The
University of the West of England.

Holly Ellis | Lighting Designer
Productions at the Finborough Theatre include *Caste*.
Trained at the London Academy of Music and Dramatic Art.
Theatre includes *Sexy Laundry* (Tabard Theatre), *Schrodinger's
Dog* (White Bear Theatre), *Communicate* (National Tour), *That
Girl* (Old Red Lion Theatre), *Sparks*, *Vanishing Man* and *Extinction
Event* (Edinburgh Festival and HighTide Festival), MA Summer
Season (East 15), *Conquest* and *Don't Panic It's Challenge Anecka*
(The Bunker), *War Plays* (Tristan Bates Theatre), *Much Ado About
Nothing*, *Twelfth Night* and *The Comedy of Errors* (Karamel Club)
and *Catherine and Anita* (King's Head Theatre and Edinburgh
Festival).
www.hollyellislighting.com

Rachael Murray | Sound Designer
Productions at the Finborough Theatre include the forthcoming *A
Lesson From Aloes*.
Trained at the Royal Academy of Dramatic Art.
Theatre includes *Drowned or Saved?*, *Screaming Secrets* and
Glass Roots (Tristan Bates Theatre), *Quietly*, *The Yellow Wallpaper*

and *The Soul of Wittgenstein* (Omnibus Theatre), *Immaculate Correction* and *Mermaids* (King's Head Theatre), *Awakening* and *No Place Like Hope* (Old Red Lion Theatre), *Woman Before a Glass* (Jermyn Street Theatre), *Gate* (Cockpit Theatre) and *House of America* (Brockley Jack Studio Theatre).

Ann Bailey | Stage Manager
Trained at East 15 Drama School.
Theatre includes *#Bestlife* (Theatre N16), *The Rise and Fall of Little Voice* (Park Theatre), *If We Go To The River, Will We See The Sea?* (Bread and Roses Theatre), *To Finally Feel* (Lion and Unicorn Theatre and Clifftown Theatre, Southend-on-Sea) and *A Clock Face Exhibition* (The Counting House).
Ann is a founding member of Brass Budgie Productions Ltd, acting as Company Stage Manager and Director of Film.

Pamela Schermann | Production Manager
Theatre includes *The Yellow Wallpaper* and T*he Soul of Wittgenstein* (Omnibus Theatre), *The Long Road South* (King's Head Theatre), *God's Waiting Room* (National Tour), *Don Giovanni* (Pleasance London) and *Polly* (Wardrobe Theatre, Bristol).
Pamela is a Creative Producer at Time Zone Theatre Ltd. She has produced plays in London venues including the Tristan Bates Theatre, Rose Playhouse and Bridewell Theatre, as well as National Tours. At the Bridewell Theatre, she has established an annual opera festival – Opera in the City Festival.

New Shoes Theatre

N E W · S H O E S
· T H E A T R E ·

New Shoes Theatre is a provocative and vibrant theatre
company which produces powerful and inspirational work
written by women.

We give a voice to women's writing and their legacy of work.
We create a multicultural and inclusive platform with
international links.
We use productions and workshops to develop theatre skills and
to involve and inspire young people.
We raise awareness about social and environmental issues.
We reach out and include marginalised groups.

Production Acknowledgements
Assistant Director | **Millie Foy**
Assistant Production Manager | **Iona Purvis**
Production Photography | **Tom Grace**
Trailer production | **Actorshack**
Set construction | **Setsmith**
Marketing | **Dave Spencer**
Artwork | **Arsalan Sattari**

Aimée Stuart biography researched and written by Nicolette Kay.

Jeannie has been funded through generous donations made by
Don Gillett and The Rivlin Family Trust.

Supported using public funding by Arts Council England National
Lottery Fund.

Thank you to The New Shoes Theatre Trustees, The Bristol
Old Vic Theatre School, WorkSpace, Ollie Kelly, Dan Simon and
Interim Spaces, G. Collins and Sons, Sofia Zervudachi, Laurence
Hughes, Cat Smyth, Megan Wilde and Anouk Chalmers.

Supported using public funding by
ARTS COUNCIL
ENGLAND
LOTTERY FUNDED

150
FINBOROUGH | THEATRE

The Finborough Theatre's building – including both the Finborough Arms pub and the Finborough Theatre – celebrates its 150th birthday in 2018.

Opened in 1868, the Finborough building was designed by one of the leading architects of his day, George Godwin (1813-1888) who was also the editor of the architectural magazine *The Builder* (which is still published today), and a sometime playwright. He is buried in nearby Brompton Cemetery.

The Finborough Arms was one of five public houses originally constructed as part of the Redcliffe Estate (which replaced the farmland and market gardens that existed before), and is one of only three pubs of the original five that still survive today.

One of the Finborough Arms' most regular customers was sanitary pioneer Thomas Crapper (1836-1910) who would would regularly begin his working day in the Finborough Arms with a bottle of champagne. His daughter, Minnie, married Ernest Finch (who was born in the flat above the theatre) of the Finch family who owned and managed the building from its opening in 1868 until the early 1930s.

FINBOROUGH | THEATRE

VIBRANT **NEW WRITING** | UNIQUE **REDISCOVERIES**

"Probably the most influential fringe theatre in the world."
Time Out

"Under Neil McPherson, possibly the most unsung of all major artistic directors in Britain, the Finborough has continued to plough a fertile path of new plays and rare revivals that gives it an influence disproportionate to its tiny 50-seat size."
Mark Shenton, The Stage 2017

"The tiny but mighty Finborough"
Ben Brantley, The New York Times

Founded in 1980 on the first floor of the building (which was previously a restaurant, a Masonic Lodge, and a billiards hall), the multi-award-winning Finborough Theatre presents plays and music theatre, concentrated exclusively on vibrant new writing and unique rediscoveries from the 19th and 20th centuries.

Our programme is unique – we never present work that has been seen anywhere in London during the last 25 years.

Do visit us our website to find out more about us, or follow us on Facebook, Twitter, Instagram, Tumblr and YouTube.

For more on the history of the building and the local area, and for full information on the Finborough Theatre's work, visit our website at **www.finboroughtheatre.co.uk**

FINBOROUGH | THEATRE

VIBRANT **NEW WRITING** | UNIQUE **REDISCOVERIES**
118 Finborough Road, London SW10 9ED
admin@finboroughtheatre.co.uk
www.finboroughtheatre.co.uk

The Finborough Theatre is a member of the Independent Theatre
Council, the Society of Independent Theatres, Musical Theatre Network,
The Friends of Brompton Cemetery and The Earl's Court Society; and
supports #time4change's Mental Health Charter.

Supported by

Mailing
Email admin@finboroughtheatre.co.uk or give your details to our
Box Office staff to join our free email list.

Feedback
We welcome your comments, complaints and suggestions. Write to
Finborough Theatre, 118 Finborough Road, London SW10 9ED or
email us at admin@finboroughtheatre.co.uk

Playscripts
Many of the Finborough Theatre's plays have been published and
are on sale from our website.

On social media

 www.facebook.com/FinboroughTheatre

 www.twitter.com/finborough

 finboroughtheatre.tumblr.com

 www.instagram.com/finboroughtheatre

 www.youtube.com/user/finboroughtheatre

Friends
The Finborough Theatre is a registered charity. We receive no public
funding, and rely solely on the support of our audiences. Please do
consider supporting us by becoming a member of our Friends of the
Finborough Theatre scheme. There are four categories of Friends,
each offering a wide range of benefits.

Friends

The Finborough Theatre is a registered charity. We receive no public funding, and rely solely on the support of our audiences. Please do consider supporting us by becoming a member of our Friends of the Finborough Theatre scheme. There are four categories of Friends, each offering a wide range of benefits.

Richard Tauber Friends – David and Melanie Alpers. David Barnes. Mark Bentley. Simon Bolland. James Carroll. Deirdre Feehan. Michael Forster. N. and D. Goldring. Loyd Grossman. Mary Hickson. Richard Jackson. Jennifer Jacobs. Paul and Lindsay Kennedy. Martin and Wendy Kramer. John Lawson. Bridget Macdougall, Kathryn McDowall. Ghazell Mitchell. Barry Serjent. Brian Smith. Lavinia Webb. Sandra Yarwood.

William Terriss Friends – Alan Godfrey. Melanie Johnson. Leo and Janet Liebster.

Adelaide Neilson Friends – Philip G Hooker.

JEANNIE

by Aimée Stuart

SAMUEL FRENCH

samuelfrench.co.uk

For Amateur Production Enquiries

United Kingdom and World
excluding North America
plays@samuelfrench.co.uk
020 7255 4302/01

Each title is subject to availability from Samuel French, depending upon country of performance.

THINKING ABOUT PERFORMING A SHOW?

There are thousands of plays and musicals available to perform from Samuel French right now, and applying for a licence is easier and more affordable than you might think

---

From classic plays to brand new musicals, from monologues to epic dramas, there are shows for everyone.

Plays and musicals are protected by copyright law, so if you want to perform them, the first thing you'll need is a licence. This simple process helps support the playwright by ensuring they get paid for their work and means that you'll have the documents you need to stage the show in public.

Not all our shows are available to perform all the time, so it's important to check and apply for a licence before you start rehearsals or commit to doing the show.

LEARN MORE & FIND THOUSANDS OF SHOWS

Browse our full range of plays and musicals, and find out more about how to license a show

www.samuelfrench.co.uk/perform

Talk to the friendly experts in our Licensing team for advice on choosing a show and help with licensing

plays@samuelfrench.co.uk   020 7387 9373

Acting Editions

BORN TO PERFORM

Playscripts designed from the ground up to work the way you do in rehearsal, performance and study

---

Larger, clearer text for easier reading

Wider margins for notes

Performance features such as character and props lists, sound and lighting cues, and more

---

+ CHOOSE A SIZE AND STYLE TO SUIT YOU

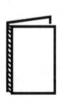

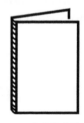

STANDARD EDITION

Our regular paperback book at our regular size

SPIRAL-BOUND EDITION

The same size as the Standard Edition, but with a sturdy, easy-to-fold, easy-to-hold spiral-bound spine

LARGE EDITION

A4 size and spiral bound, with larger text and a blank page for notes opposite every page of text – perfect for technical and directing use

LEARN MORE | **samuelfrench.co.uk/actingeditions**

AUTHOR'S NOTE

The Austrian waiter can speak broken English instead of German.

MUSIC USE NOTE

Licensees are solely responsible for obtaining formal written permission from copyright owners to use copyrighted music in the performance of this play and are strongly cautioned to do so. If no such permission is obtained by the licensee, then the licensee must use only original music that the licensee owns and controls. Licensees are solely responsible and liable for all music clearances and shall indemnify the copyright owners of the play(s) and their licensing agent, Samuel French, against any costs, expenses, losses and liabilities arising from the use of music by licensees. Please contact the appropriate music licensing authority in your territory for the rights to any incidental music.

IMPORTANT BILLING AND CREDIT REQUIREMENTS

If you have obtained performance rights to this title, please refer to your licensing agreement for important billing and credit requirements.

JEANNIE

Jeannie produced at the Torch Theatre, London, on February 6th, 1940, and subsequently played at Wyndham's Theatre, London, on April 3rd, 1940, with the following cast of characters:

FATHER ....James Woodburn
JEANNIE .... Barbara Mullen
MRS. WHITELAW ....Dorothy Hamilton
BESSIE.................................... Eleanor Wilson
MAGGIE...................................... Diana Caird
STANLEY SMITH............................... Eric Portman
PORTER ....James Page
ATTENDANT..................................Thomas Dance
RECEPTION CLERK ....Olaf Olsen
THE BLONDE .... Tatiana Lieven
THE COUNT .... Albert Lieven
HOTEL WAITER .... Leo de Pokorny
PAGE ....John Valentine
SMALLER PAGE .... Dane Gordon
AN AMERICAN (1ST)............................ Ilona Ference
AN AMERICAN (2ND) ....Joy Erskine Young
WAITER .... Victor Fairley
THE MISTRESS...........................Beatrix Feilden-Kaye
HER HUSBAND..................................James Page

The Play produced by Irene Hentschel.

CHARACTERS

FATHER

JEANNIE

MRS. WHITELAW

BESSIE

MAGGIE

STANLEY SMITH

PORTER

ATTENDANT

RECEPTION CLERK

THE BLONDE

THE COUNT

HOTEL WAITER

PAGE

SMALLER PAGE

AN AMERICAN (1ST)

AN AMERICAN (2ND)

WAITER

THE MISTRESS

HER HUSBAND

SYNOPSIS OF SCENES

ACT I

ACT II

ACT III

ACT I

Scene One

SCENE—A part of the kitchen of a small grey stone house in a small grey village in Scotland.

This kitchen is also a living-room, scullery, wash-house and bedroom. The impression we get is cheerful. Everything is spotlessly clean. There are muslin screens on the small windows—looking out on to the back-green where the washing is hanging out to dry. The side curtains are of cretonne. We should see the clothes-line—stretched between two stationary poles and held up at intervals by props cleft at the top end. In a semi-alcove is a boiler—a stone receptacle lined with zinc—with a little opening for a fire underneath. This is where the clothes are boiled. Everything seems to have been planned to make housework difficult and laborious. There are a kitchen table—the wood scrubbed till it is almost white—kitchen chairs, a "grandfather" chair, a rocking-chair, a shelf holding the china in daily use—some of it old and beautiful, some of it cheap odd pieces bought when necessary from the oddment basket of the local shop. The walls are papered except round the sink and the boiler, where they are washed a crude blue. The floor is of stone, scrubbed clean. Patchwork rugs are laid in front of the grate and the windows. A door leads to a little porch with growing plants in it. This opens on to the street, and also leads to a narrow stair. Another door opens to the back-green.

When the curtain rises FATHER *is discovered sitting right of the table. He is reading the family Bible.*

MRS. WHITELAW *(offstage)* Jeannie! *(She knocks)* Jeannie! *(She opens the door and comes in left*—sees FATHER *when she had expected* JEANNIE*)* Oh! *(She recovers)* Good afternoon, Mr. McLean. Is Jeannie at 'ome? *(She carries a milk-jug. We hear the sound of her wireless dance music)*

FATHER *(shows his dislike of her)* Whaur wad she be if she wisna?

MRS. WHITELAW Pardon? *(Left of the table)*

FATHER I said, "Whaur wad she be if she wisna?"

MRS. WHITELAW *(giggles)* I'm ever so sorry, Mr. McLean, but I can't understand a word you say.

FATHER That's nae loss tae me, Mistress Whitelaw.

MRS. WHITELAW Where's Jeannie?

FATHER She's ben washing her face after a hard day's work, which is more than you've done, by the looks of you.

MRS. WHITELAW That's right. I don't believe in working *my* fingers to the bone.

FATHER Onyone could see that. What does the guid book say, "Go to the ant, thou sluggard, consider her ways and be wise." *(He puts the book on the table)*

MRS. WHITELAW Oh!

FATHER What dae ye want with he.

MRS. WHITELAW I just looked in to ask if she could let me 'ave a drop of milk for Angus's tea.

FATHER Whaur's yer ain?

MRS. WHITELAW Pardon?

FATHER I said, "Whaur's yer ain?"

MRS. WHITELAW Oh—my own? The cat knocked it over.

FATHER It shouldna have been whaur the cat could get at it.

MRS. WHITELAW It was that fool of a milkman went and left it on the ledge outside the kitchen window whilst I was 'aving me afternoon nap.

FATHER *(disgusted)* Afternoon nap! A great sonsy creature like you! Ye ought tae be ashamed of yersel'.

MRS. WHITELAW Why shouldn't I 'ave me bit of shut-eye if I 'ave a mind to? *(She holds out a jug)* Oh, be matey and lend me a drop till to-morrow morning, there's a dear.

FATHER *(furious at the endearment)* I neither lend nor borrow.

MRS. WHITELAW All right—all right—I'll buy it off of you, then. 'Ow's that?

FATHER That's different. *(He rises)* But ye'll require tae pay through the nose for your carelessness. How much dae ye require?

MRS. WHITELAW A penn'orth'll do.

FATHER *(crosses to the chest of drawers)* I'll charge ye tuppence for it. That'll learn ye.

MRS. WHITELAW Reely, Mr. McLean, you are a smartie and no mistake! A person'd 'ave to be up early to put it acrost you.

FATHER Aye, would they? Gie us yer jug. *(He takes it from her and measures out a small quantity of milk)*

MRS. WHITELAW *dances a few steps to the wireless music.*

And while we're at it, I'll thank ye tae stop turning on that wireless contraption of yours from furst thing in the morning tae last thing at night.

MRS. WHITELAW I must 'ave somethink to pass the time.

FATHER If ye wis tae dae yer duty by yer husband the time wad pass soon enough. Ye've been marrit nine months and whit hae ye tae show for it?

MRS. WHITELAW *(giggles)* Reely, Mr. McLean, wot will you say next? *(She moves to left of the rocking-chair)*

FATHER Whaur's yer tuppence?

MRS. WHITELAW *(giving him twopence from her pocket)* 'Ere you are—

FATHER And there's yer milk.

MRS. WHITELAW Thanks ever so. You *are* kind.

FATHER Now mak' yersel' scarce.

MRS. WHITELAW Right you are, ducks! Keep your 'air on! *(She goes to the door left)* See you again soon. *(When she is safely at the door)* Naughty—naughty!

MRS. WHITELAW *exits left.*

FATHER *(almost speechless with rage)* Brazen limmer! *(He moves up to the window, putting the Bible on the chest of drawers on his way up)*

Suddenly the brilliant sunshine clouds over. There is a gust of wind, followed by a downpour of rain. The poles holding the clothes-line up are blown down. The sheets fall to the ground. FATHER, *at the window, watches this with angry satisfaction, then turns his head and calls.*

Jeannie! *(No answer. Moving right to below the table)* Jeannie—!

JEANNIE *(from above)* Aye?

FATHER Here!

JEANNIE What is it?

FATHER Cam doon here a minute.

JEANNIE I can't. I'm changing my dress.

FATHER Dae as yer telt! Cam here, I say.

JEANNIE Bother! You'll need to wait.

FATHER Do you hear me speaking to you?

JEANNIE Can you no give me a minute's peace? What is it?

JEANNIE appears at the door right. Her hair is screwed back unbecomingly. She is putting on her cardigan as she comes in.

FATHER Your sheets.

JEANNIE What about ma sheets?

FATHER They're doon. *(Right of the table)*

JEANNIE Down? *(Below the table—looking up stage and out of the window—sees the tragedy. The next words are wrung from her heart)* Oh, my, ma sheets!

JEANNIE darts to the door left and out. FATHER puffs.

FATHER *(calls)* Have you rescued them?

JEANNIE Aye.

FATHER Are they a' there?

JEANNIE Aye.

FATHER Are they a' right?

JEANNIE enters, carrying the damp sheets in a zinc tub. If JEANNIE were the crying sort she would be in tears when she re-enters.

JEANNIE No.

FATHER *(watching anxiously)* Are they torn?

JEANNIE *(crossing to the boiler right)* No. They're dirtied.

FATHER *(relieved)* That doesna matter.

JEANNIE *(kneels and puts the tub on the floor below the boiler, examining the sheets)* Doesn't it? That's all you care. I'll need to do them all over again.

FATHER So long as they're not torn.

JEANNIE *(after a short silence)* Did you not see it coming on? *(Rising, putting on her overall which was hanging on the door right)*

FATHER Aye.

JEANNIE Why didn't you call me in time?

FATHER I did. You wouldna come.

JEANNIE I would if you'd said. It's the pink limit.

FATHER *(angrily)* Dinna use swear words!

JEANNIE *(kneeling and lifting the dirty end of a sheet and examining it)* What else will I use?

FATHER I'll no hae bad language—not in this house. If you want to swear you can go somewhere else.

JEANNIE I wish I could.

FATHER What's that?

JEANNIE I said I wish I could. I'd give my soul to get out of this. Aye, and out of this one-eyed wee town!

FATHER Is that what she calls it? *(Vindictively)* That English hussy. She's leading you astray.

JEANNIE *(with a bitter laugh, gets soap and kneels on the floor, soaping the sheets)* Leading me astray? Here?

FATHER You were quite content with your lot before she came on the scene.

JEANNIE Was I? That's all you know.

FATHER Since Angus Whitelaw was daft enough to marry on her you've not been the same lassie.

JEANNIE *(bitterly)* Lassie! D'you mind how old I am?

FATHER Age disna matter. You're a lass till you're a wife.

JEANNIE What opportunity have I had to be a wife? There's not an unmarried man in the place. Not that I'd have him if there were.

FATHER "Chance is a fine thing." *(He goes up to the dresser for his tobacco)*

JEANNIE That's what I've never had—a chance.

FATHER Talk sense.

JEANNIE I am talking sense. I've not had a holiday since Mother died.

FATHER You get a day in Glasgow two-three times a year.

JEANNIE What can you do in a day?

FATHER As much as is good for you. *(Crossing to sit right of the table—lights his pipe)*

JEANNIE *(who has been trying to get the dirtied parts of the sheets clean, puts the soap on the boiler)* Uch, I'll need to boil them again! *(She gets paper and sticks from the stove and starts to rake out the grate under the boiler)*

FATHER Go canny with the sticks. *(A pause)* Did you keep the big ashes?

Enter MRS. WHITELAW from down left, wearing a hat and coat and carrying a mackintosh, umbrella, gloves and handbag.

MRS. WHITELAW 'Ullo!

JEANNIE Hullo—

FATHER Whit dae ye want to borrow this time?

MRS. WHITELAW Nothing. Nor to buy anything neither.

JEANNIE *(turns on her knees to MRS. WHITELAW and FATHER)* Ye havena *sold* something to Mistress Whitelaw?

FATHER And whit if I have? She's for ever asking ye tae lend her things.

JEANNIE *(shocked)* She always pays me back.

FATHER Aye—short measure. If ye lend her the big end of the loaf, she pays ye back the wee end; if ye lend her a heaped cup of flour she pays ye back a flat one—

JEANNIE *(to* MRS. WHITELAW*)* What did he sell you?

MRS. WHITELAW On'y a drop of milk for Angus's tea.

JEANNIE Fancy charging you for it. *(To* FATHER*)* What would Mother have said?

FATHER *(rising)* Yer mother wad hae mair sense than tae say onything—aye, nor tae tak up wi' a bissom like her. *(He crosses to the door left)*

JEANNIE   } *(together)* { Father—!
MRS. WHITELAW }   { Oh, manners—manners!

FATHER Jezebel!

He flings a coat from the pegs over his shoulder, nearly catching MRS. WHITELAW, *and exits left.*

MRS. WHITELAW *moves to the table.*

JEANNIE *(a step to* MRS. WHITELAW*)* I'm sorry. I'm awful affronted. You'll need to take no notice. *(She turns and puts a shovel of coal into the boiler)*

MRS. WHITELAW *(sits on the table)* That's all right. Don't worry. I can look after myself. What are you doing?

JEANNIE I'm at ma sheets. *(She goes on working)*

MRS. WHITELAW At this time of day? I thought I saw you hanging them out this morning.

JEANNIE You did. The storm blew them down.

MRS. WHITELAW What a shame!

JEANNIE *(glancing round and seeing that her* FATHER *has gone)* Shame? It's the pink limit! If there's one thing I hate washing—it's sheets! *(Twisting round to the sheets)*

MRS. WHITELAW Why don't you send them to the laundry? I do.

JEANNIE I'd like to see Father's face if I suggested it.

MRS. WHITELAW Angus didn't like it at first. I put my foot down.

JEANNIE It's well seen you can!

MRS. WHITELAW He said his mother always did them herself. I said I wasn't his mother. It's the only thing to do—to begin the way you mean to go on. My mum gave me the tip. The night before my wedding she came to my room and said, "I'm not going to tell you the facts of life. You'll find them out soon enough. But I'll give you a piece of useful advice. Get your own way from the start or you'll not get it afterwards." *(A short pause)* I'm off to the pictures.

JEANNIE *(rising and drying her hands on the roller towel)* You're lucky. You're always off to the pictures.

MRS. WHITELAW What else is there to do in this one-eyed town? Must have a bit of fun once in a while. I looked in to see if you'd come with me?

JEANNIE *(moving towards* MRS. WHITELAW*)* I wish I could.

MRS. WHITELAW Come on, then.

JEANNIE How can I? I'm at my sheets.

MRS. WHITELAW Leave them in soak.

JEANNIE Uch! I can't.

MRS. WHITELAW Why not?

JEANNIE Father doesn't care about me going to a cinema.

MRS. WHITELAW Don't tell him. Say you're going for a walk.

JEANNIE I can't do that.

MRS. WHITELAW Why not?

JEANNIE It'd be a lie.

MRS. WHITELAW *(powdering her face)* No, it wouldn't. You'll have to walk there and back. Anyway, what's a lie more or less?

JEANNIE I'm a stickler for the truth. *(A pause)* I'd require to ask for the money. *(A step or so to right)*

MRS. WHITELAW Take it out of the housekeeping.

JEANNIE I don't get any housekeeping. He doles out just what we need. *(She turns towards* MRS. WHITELAW*)*

MRS. WHITELAW Good heavens! I wouldn't put up with that.

JEANNIE If you'd Father, you'd just need to. He's always done it. With my Mother as well.

MRS. WHITELAW I'd see Angus far enough first! Wait a tick till I look in my bag. Perhaps I've enough for us both. *(She looks in her purse)*

JEANNIE *(hastily)* I can't let you pay for me.

MRS. WHITELAW Why not?

JEANNIE I can't accept what I can't return.

MRS. WHITELAW Go on. Don't be so proud.

JEANNIE I'm not proud. But I hate a sponger.

MRS. WHITELAW *(closing her purse)* Anyhow, I haven't got it. To-morrow's pay-day. That settles it.

JEANNIE It was settled already. Thanks all the same. *(She turns to the fireplace)*

MRS. WHITELAW *(rising)* Well, I suppose if you can't come, you can't. What's the time? *(She glances at her wrist-watch)*

JEANNIE *looks at her enviously.*

Twenty to six. I must fly! Don't want to miss anything! *(Moving to the door left)*

JEANNIE *(weakening)* What's on? Is it a good programme?

MRS. WHITELAW *(moving centre—left of* JEANNIE*)* Clark and Myrna. *(Or the he-man of the moment)* Here's the leaflet with a picture. *(She shows it—they gaze at it together)* Oh, I wish someone'd kiss me like that!

JEANNIE *(looking at the leaflet)* You have a husband.

MRS. WHITELAW They don't do it when you're married to them. *(Putting the leaflet away and moving left)* Ta-ta.

JEANNIE *(unable to resist, stops her)* Will you wait a minute?

FATHER *is seen outside the window. Sits on the chair beneath the window outside.*

MRS. WHITELAW What for?

JEANNIE Just till I see if I can get the money out of Father. I could do with a bit of romance to-night—if it's only a picture.

MRS. WHITELAW Good for you.

JEANNIE *moves up right of the table to the window,* MRS. WHITELAW *moves up left of the table to the window.*

JEANNIE Father!

FATHER Aye?

JEANNIE Will you be all right for a wee while?

FATHER Why? *(Suspiciously)* Where are you going?

JEANNIE Out.

FATHER What for? *(Who has been sitting on the chair outside the window, rises)*

JEANNIE A wee walk.

FATHER Who with?

JEANNIE Mistress Whitelaw.

FATHER *(to MRS. WHITELAW—through the window)* "She is loud and stubborn, her feet abide not in her house."

JEANNIE *(lowering her voice, anxiously)* Whisht, Father!

FATHER I'll no whisht! I'm not going to put up with it any longer. *(As he walks away)* The sooner she stops coming to this house, the better.

JEANNIE It's no use! *(She crosses to the fireplace)*

MRS. WHITELAW *(crosses to left of JEANNIE)* Go on, stick up for yourself—

FATHER *(appearing in the doorway left)* What's all this nonsense?

JEANNIE *(swallowing her retort)* I'll need ninepence.

FATHER What for?

JEANNIE To spend.

FATHER What on?

JEANNIE Uch, stop asking questions! I'm in a hurry.

FATHER She's asked you to go to the cinema.

JEANNIE What if she has?

FATHER You're not going, that's what!

JEANNIE Why not?

FATHER Hotbeds of vice. I never went to one. Neither did your mother.

JEANNIE How do you know they're hotbeds of vice if you never went to one?

FATHER I know in more than you think.

JEANNIE Come on, Father! *(She crosses to him left)*

FATHER Haud your tongue. Dae ye ken who you're speaking to?

JEANNIE Come on, be a sport. I must have a bit of fun, once in a while.

FATHER What for dae ye want fan at your age?

JEANNIE Because I've never had it. Come on. I canna keep Mistress Whitelaw waiting any longer.

FATHER Let her go, and good riddance. *(He crosses to centre between the two women)* Mistress Whitelaw, once and for all I'll thank ye not to bring your English ungodly notions into this house. I'll not hae my lassie forget she's been brought up in the fear of the Lord. You and your cinemas and your high heels and your low necks! You shameless faggot! *(He crosses to the door left)*

JEANNIE *Whisht,* Father—!

FATHER I'll no whisht. And I'll no gie ye good money tae squander on Godless fun.

He exits left.

MRS. WHITELAW Mean old skunk!

JEANNIE Mistress Whitelaw, I'll thank ye not to speak that way about my father. *(By the rocking-chair)*

MRS. WHITELAW I wouldn't have your life—not for the world! I'd sooner be a servant.

JEANNIE *(shocked)* A servant, me?

MRS. WHITELAW It's what you are now. *(She moves to right centre)* Only you don't get paid for it. You could get a pound a week and an evening off and every second Sunday and a whole day a month. *And* you could refuse to wash sheets.

JEANNIE It sounds like Paradise.

MRS. WHITELAW I don't know about Paradise. But it'd be a darn sight better than this.

JEANNIE I *am* my own mistress. *(She sits in the rocking-chair)*

MRS. WHITELAW *(centre)* D'you call this being your own mistress? I call it slavery.

JEANNIE Whatever you call it, I'll just need to go on with it.

MRS. WHITELAW Why?

JEANNIE How can I leave Father at his age?

MRS. WHITELAW Let your cousins in Glasgow take a turn.

JEANNIE How can they? They can't leave their husbands.

MRS. WHITELAW Let him go to them.

JEANNIE They've no room. They've only got wee flats. Besides, he'd never do it. He's lived here all his life. He's too old to change now.

MRS. WHITELAW How old is he?

JEANNIE Seventy-two.

MRS. WHITELAW Angus says he'll live to be a hundred. Another twenty-eight years.

JEANNIE You're good at arithmetic.

MRS. WHITELAW Fancy going on like this for another twenty-eight years. My God! *(A slight turn away right)*

JEANNIE Mistress Whitelaw, if you want to use bad language, will you please go elsewhere?

MRS. WHITELAW Call that bad language? If I said what I'd like to say, you'd hear something.

FATHER *is seen sitting outside the window.*

JEANNIE *(coldly)* You'll need to away, if you don't want to miss the first kiss.

MRS. WHITELAW Keep your hair on! I'm going. *(She crosses down left to the door)* You're a fool to waste your life on a mean, bad-tempered old man. *(She looks towards the porch)* I don't care who hears me say it! *(To* **JEANNIE***)* Ta-ta! Sorry you can't come. Good luck to your sheets!

Exit **MRS. WHITELAW** *left.*

JEANNIE *(rises—crosses right, pours water from the pail into the boiler—takes the sheets, pushes them in, takes her stick and pokes viciously at the sheets)* Get into the water with you! Go on! Get in!

Curtain.

Scene Two

SCENE—The same, three months later. There is certain rearrangement of furniture, noted at the end of the text of the play.

When the curtain rises we see two young women dressed cheaply but smartly in black. The kettle is on the fire. MAGGIE *is at the stove trying the heat of her curling-tongs on a piece of paper which she screws up and throws away.* BESSIE *is polishing her shoe with a duster at the window. At first there is a dour silence: then* BESSIE *turns from the window and goes on with the argument.*

BESSIE It's no use, Maggie, I'm not having her to live with me.

MAGGIE *(lowers her voice)* Whisht! She'll hear you.

BESSIE She can't. She's away at the cemetery, planting flowers on the grave.

MAGGIE Why should I have her? *(She crosses to right of the table)*

BESSIE Why should *I*?

MAGGIE You've got a spare room. *(Curling her hair with the tongs)*

BESSIE Colin's cousin's coming next week.

MAGGIE *(stirring the tea, putting the lid and cosy on again)* Why should you have Colin's cousin and not your own?

BESSIE Only on a visit. If I had Jeannie I'd never get rid of her.

MAGGIE Neither would I. *(She sits right of the table and continues business with pocket mirror from her handbag which she puts on the table and continues to curl her hair)*

BESSIE She could help you with the kids. *(Knows this is the best argument. She moves to above the table)* You'd be able to get out at nights with Bob. And to the Rugger matches on Saturday afternoons.

MAGGIE *(weakening)* I'd like that part all right. Where would she sleep?

BESSIE You could put the cupboard-bed back in the kitchen.

MAGGIE Bob wouldn't like that. He likes to be alone when he shaves.

BESSIE *takes a sweet from* MAGGIE*'s open handbag.* MAGGIE *pushes away her hand and helps herself. They both suck sweets.*

You'd need to take her half-time.

BESSIE If only she didn't look such a sight! That lanky hair! *(Grossing to left of the table)*

MAGGIE She could have it permed.

BESSIE Would she? She's that old-fashioned! Not even a dab of powder on her nose. Heaven knows it needs it! *(She sits left of the table)*

MAGGIE It's not a bad wee nose.

BESSIE It's bright red.

MAGGIE Go on. Don't exaggerate. I admit it's shiny. If only she'd get married. *(Cleaning her nails with an orange-stick)*

BESSIE Married? Who'd have her?

MAGGIE Plainer girls than her get a husband.

BESSIE She's too old.

MAGGIE How old is she?

BESSIE Thirty-one. I saw it last night in the big Bible.

MAGGIE She's got her two hundred pounds. *(A pause. She makes up her mind)* No. No, I can't do it. That hair and that nose for breakfast, dinner and tea!

BESSIE *does business of easing tight shoes.*

I'd go dotty. She's nothing to say for herself.

The door is flung open. JEANNIE, *dressed in severe and unbecoming black, stands in the doorway right, carrying a coat and a small purse.*

JEANNIE *(her words coming breathlessly)* Oh, hasn't she, though? That's where you make a mistake. *(Crossing to pegs above the door left)*

MAGGIE *(aghast)* Jeannie!

JEANNIE Aye, Jeannie's my name. *(Hanging her coat on the pegs)*

MAGGIE I thought you were away at the cemetery planting flowers on the grave.

JEANNIE *(puts her purse in the top drawer of the chest of drawers)* I was. I'm back. *(A short pause)* I may's well tell you I've heard every word. *(Above the table)*

BESSIE *(whose best defence is attack)* Were you listening at the keyhole?

JEANNIE You know I wasn't. I didn't need to. I was in my bedroom.

BESSIE You might have had the decency to let us know.

JEANNIE Well, I hadn't. And I'm glad. Now I'll answer you. First let me start with my nose. If you lived where there was as much east wind, yours would be red too. As for powder: I'd like Father to have caught me using it. He'd have taken his stick to me. As for that stuff you put on your lips, I was ashamed of you at the funeral. You look like a pair of totties, both of you.

MAGGIE *and* BESSIE *show outraged indignation.*

And as for me having nothing to say for myself; if you'd spent your life in this one-eyed wee town your conversation'd have worn a bit thin.

BESSIE You shouldn't have stayed.

JEANNIE Someone had to look after Father. You all took it for granted it would be me. *(A pause)* As you say, I'm thirty-one.

P'raps that is a bit too old to get married, but you'll be surprised to hear it's not too old to enjoy myself. And I'm going to—if it takes the whole of my two hundred pounds.

MAGGIE } *(together)* { Jeannie!
BESSIE }   { Jeannie!

JEANNIE As I told you before, Jeannie's my name. *(She sits above the table)*

MAGGIE What on earth do you mean?

JEANNIE What I say. It's the first time I've had any money of my own. I'm going to spend it.

BESSIE Have you taken leave of your wits?

JEANNIE *(an affirmative)* Maybe!

MAGGIE What will you do when your money's all gone?

JEANNIE I'm going as a servant.

BESSIE *(shocked to the core)* A servant? You can't do that!

JEANNIE Can't I, though? It's what I've been all along. I've done every blessed thing in this house for the last fifteen years.

BESSIE That's not the same.

JEANNIE No. I didn't get paid for it. Now I will. I'll get a pound a week and an evening off and every second Sunday and a whole day a month. And I can refuse to wash sheets.

BESSIE You'll need to call yourself a housekeeper.

JEANNIE Why?

BESSIE I wouldn't like Colin's family to get to know I'd a cousin a servant.

JEANNIE What do I care about Colin's family? A fat lot they'd do for me. Not that I want them to!

BESSIE *(annoyed)* Well, I—

MAGGIE How are you going to set about enjoying yourself?

JEANNIE I'm going on a holiday.

MAGGIE Where to?

JEANNIE The world.

MAGGIE What part of the world?

JEANNIE As much of it as I can get for the money. My first stop's Vienna. *(Leaning forward on the table)*

BESSIE Vienna? Why Vienna?

JEANNIE I've heard the Blue Danube on Mistress Whitelaw's wireless. I want to hear it played at the source.

A pause.

BESSIE It'll be an awful dear fare.

JEANNIE That's nothing to me. I'm going to chuck money about for a change. I like to think it was Father's. That'll add to the fun.

Another short pause.

BESSIE Well, I suppose if you've made up your mind, it's no use trying to argue.

JEANNIE None at all. *(She hears a sniffle)* What's the matter with you, Maggie?

MAGGIE *(crying)* I'm sorry that you overheard what we said.

JEANNIE I'm not. It's put me on my mettle.

MAGGIE It's not that we're not fond of you. It's just that Bob— *(She rises and sits in the rocking-chair)*

JEANNIE Here—stop crying about it.

MAGGIE It's just that Bob—

JEANNIE *(rising—to MAGGIE)* I know. No man wants his wife's relations. I understand. *(To the chair right of the table)* The only thing I mind is what you said about my nose. I've always thought it my best feature.

BESSIE So it would be, if you gave it half a chance. You scrub it as if it was a bit of linoleum. No one uses soap on their face nowadays. Ladies that value their complexions don't even use water.

JEANNIE The dirty things! How do they get clean?

BESSIE Cleansing cream and lotion.

JEANNIE Sounds rotten to me. I hope I'll never sink so low as not to wash my face.

MAGGIE *(an alarmed exclamation)* Just look at the time! Did you ever!

BESSIE fetches her hat and coat from the pegs and crosses above the table to the fireplace.

(to JEANNIE*)* Do you think we can catch the train? *(Over to her hat and coat hanging on the pegs, crossing below the table)*

JEANNIE Easy.

MAGGIE *(putting on her hat and coat)* Thank heaven for that! Bob'll be mad if I'm not back for his tea.

JEANNIE Are you packed?

MAGGIE My pyjamas are in my coat pocket. *(Indicating the pyjamas)*

BESSIE *(who is putting on her hat and coat)* Where's mine?

JEANNIE I put them in this drawer. *(She goes to chest of drawers—remembers)* Oh, aye, here. *(Finds pyjamas)* Seems awful funny-like, girls wearing pyjamas— 'specially when they're married. *(They are amused)* What are you laughing at? *(Moving centre above the table)*

BESSIE *(who has exchanged a look with* MAGGIE*)* You do say daft things!

JEANNIE *(holding up legs)* It's you that's daft. *(She gives them to* BESSIE*)*

MAGGIE *sits left of the table.*

Would you like a paper bag?

BESSIE *(stuffing the pyjamas in her coat pocket)* I wouldn't be seen dead with a paper bag!

JEANNIE Why not? What's wrong with a nice clean paper bag?

BESSIE Oh, well, if you don't know any better.

JEANNIE Oh, here, I was forgetting the main thing. Where's my purse? *(She finds it in the dresser drawer)* I've got a ten-shilling note each for you to buy something you don't need. *(She finds the notes)*

MAGGIE Oh no, Jeannie. We can't take them. *(She rises and backs round to back of the chair)*

JEANNIE Go on. It's the first time I've been able to give anything to anyone. I'll be hurt if you refuse.

MAGGIE If you really mean it?

JEANNIE I do. *(She hands a note to* MAGGIE—*a step nearer* MAGGIE*)*

MAGGIE *(taking the note)* Thanks. It's very kind of you. I need some stockings.

JEANNIE I should think you do, with the rubbish you wear. Like tissue-paper. Here's yours, Bessie. *(She hands it to* BESSIE*)*

BESSIE *(collecting her bag from the rocking-chair and putting on the hat)* Thanks. Just put it on the table, will you?

JEANNIE *(with a look at* BESSIE, *she puts the note on the right end of the table and turns again to* MAGGIE*)* And here's a new thripp'ny-bit each for Elizabeth and wee Margaret Rose.

MAGGIE Thanks. What nice new ones.

JEANNIE I got them spesh'lly.

MAGGIE I'll put them in their savings bank.

JEANNIE No. Don't do that. Give it them to spend how they like. When I was wee I always wanted to spend how I liked. I never got doing it.

BESSIE *(finishes her toilet, crosses to above the armchair, takes up the ten-shilling note avd stuffs it into her bag; speaking with a sudden spurt of energy)* Come on, if you're coming! Bye-bye, Jeannie. *(She crosses below the table and out left)*

JEANNIE Good-bye.

MAGGIE Good-bye. *(She kisses JEANNIE)*

JEANNIE Good-bye.

MAGGIE If you've got time, send us a postcard of Vienna.

JEANNIE I'll have time all right.

MAGGIE Well, good-bye, and be good. *(She crosses to the door left)* If you can't be good, be careful.

JEANNIE I'm always careful.

BESSIE *(through the window)* Try using powder and lipstick.

Exit MAGGIE left.

JEANNIE That's one thing I'll not do. Good-bye.

BESSIE
MAGGIE } *(through the window)* { Good-bye.

JEANNIE Bye-bye!

BESSIE *and* MAGGIE *are gone. When her cousins are out of sight* JEANNIE *turns back into the kitchen. She fetches a small mirror from the top drawer in the chest of drawers, sits above the table, gazes intently at her reflection in the mirror—touches her nose—as though to alter its shape—looks up and out.*

(looking at herself again) I'll just need to be good!

Curtain.

Scene Three

SCENE—The rail and a small piece of deck of a Channel boat. There is harbour noise; also chains. A siren and the voice of sea-gulls.

When the curtain rises: STANLEY SMITH *discovered; he is a short, squarely-built man—is standing with an arm on the rail, idly watching activities. We hear the confused noises of a ship about to depart. If possible, we see* PORTERS *and Passengers.*

JEANNIE *(off stage, in an agitated voice)* My luggage! I can't go without my luggage! Here, wait a minute. Don't take down the gangway—I can't go without my luggage!

STANLEY SMITH *glances towards the voice. He smiles to himself.* JEANNIE, *making for the gangway, appears, looking agitated. She now wears the jacket belonging to the skirt we saw her in last, and a neat black hat and black gloves. She carries a black handbag and a rolled-up umbrella. She speaks as she comes in sight.*

—I'll require to get off— *(She crosses* STANLEY*)*

STANLEY *(left, steps forward, raises his hat, speaks with an unmistakable Yorkshire accent)* Excuse me. Can I be of any assistance?

JEANNIE *(scarcely sparing time to glance at him)* Yes, you can. The boat's just going to start and I can't find my luggage.

STANLEY What did you do with it?

JEANNIE A porter yanked it out of my grasp.

STANLEY *(quickly hiding a smile)* What's his number?

JEANNIE His number? I don't know. He said he'd meet me on deck.

STANLEY Didn't he give you a ticket?

JEANNIE No.

STANLEY What's this in your hand? *(He takes the ticket from her)*

JEANNIE Have I had it in my hand all the time?

STANLEY Looks like it. *(He holds the ticket at a distance— long-sightedly—reads)* Number Ninety-seven. *(He looks round, calls)* Hi there! Number Ninety-seven! Number Ninety-seven! *(He crosses* JEANNIE *to call to the* PORTER *off right)*

PORTER *(offstage)* Yes, sir?

The PORTER *comes into view.*

Here, sir!

STANLEY Where's this lady's luggage?

PORTER Over there, sir. Under that seat.

STANLEY Why didn't you let her know?

PORTER I did, sir. She wouldn't take any notice.

JEANNIE I didn't understand. *(She looks off, anxiously)* Is my hold-all there, too?

PORTER Yes, miss. Behind the basket.

JEANNIE Thank you. *(She opens the handbag—crossing in front of* STANLEY *to the* PORTER) What do I owe you?

PORTER I leave that to you, miss.

JEANNIE *(searching agitatedly in her bag)* Uch, where's my purse? There's such a lot in my bag. I can't find it.

STANLEY Don't worry about it just now. I'll see to this.

JEANNIE Thank you. I'll settle up with you later. *(With new agitation; to the* PORTER) You'll require to get off.

PORTER That's all right, miss. I could do with a little 'oliday.

JEANNIE What about your wife? She'll be keeping your dinner hot.

PORTER Not much fear of that, mum. My wife don't open the tin till she 'ears me fairy footsteps on the stair!

JEANNIE *(shocked)* Does she give you tinned stuff for your dinner?

PORTER She does, miss.

JEANNIE That's not fair!

PORTER That's what I tell 'er, miss.

JEANNIE You must be firm with her.

A ship's bell.

Hurry up! You'll be too late!

PORTER Right this time, miss. I'll 'ave to sprint for it. Good day, sir.

STANLEY crosses to the PORTER, gives him a coin, then he crosses behind JEANNIE.

(taking it) Thank you, sir. Good day, miss. Good luck to you.

Exit the PORTER.

JEANNIE Same to you! Good-bye! *(She watches the PORTER out of sight)* Will he manage it? *(A pause while she follows his movements)* My, that was quick work! *(She waves)* Good-bye! Good luck! And don't forget, be firm with her! *(She waves—looks a moment or two longer, then turns to STANLEY)* How much did you give him?

STANLEY Half a crown.

JEANNIE *(shocked)* Half a crown? *(She looks at STANLEY directly for the first time)*

STANLEY If you think it too much, give me what you'd have given yourself.

JEANNIE No, indeed. I must pay my debts. You just took me by surprise, that's all. *(She hands STANLEY half a crown)* Here. *(As STANLEY hesitates)* Go on—I can afford it.

STANLEY If you insist.

JEANNIE I do.

STANLEY *(taking the coin)* Thanks.

JEANNIE *(with dignity)* It's me that should thank you. I'm much obliged. *(She unbends)* It was awful silly-like, making that mistake. He kept on telling me he was Number Ninety-seven. I thought he was being rude.

STANLEY *guffaws.*

Why do you laugh?

STANLEY Sorry! I— *(Controlling himself)* —I'm not used to the Scotch accent.

JEANNIE Have I got an accent?

A siren.

(with excitement) Oh, look! We're away! *(She crosses left)*

If you'll excuse me, I'll get where I can see everything. Thank you again for your kindness. Good-bye. *(She goes quickly left, her eyes full of excitement)*

STANLEY *watches her with a smile, and raises his hat.*

Curtain.

Scene Four

SCENE—The dining compartment of a Continental express train. The table is set for dinner.

When the curtain rises, for the moment the compartment is empty. JEANNIE *comes in down right, looking wan and uncertain, from the corridor. The* ATTENDANT, *down left, is laying the table. He sees* JEANNIE *and comes to her.*

ATTENDANT Dinner is not served yet, madame.

JEANNIE I'll just sit and wait.

ATTENDANT *(holding out his hand)* The ticket, if you please, madame.

JEANNIE What ticket? *(She sits right of the table)*

ATTENDANT For the first service, madame. With the number of the place.

JEANNIE I haven't got one.

ATTENDANT I am afraid madame must wait for the second service.

JEANNIE When's that?

ATTENDANT Eight o'clock.

JEANNIE Eight o'clock? That's an hour and a half! Could you not let me have a cup of tea?

ATTENDANT I regret, madame. All places are reserved in advance.

JEANNIE What a nuisance! Will I require a ticket for the second service?

ATTENDANT No, madame. For the second service there is always a place.

JEANNIE How will I know? *(She rises)*

ATTENDANT An attendant comes to each compartment, madame.

Exit the ATTENDANT *left.*

JEANNIE Thank you.

JEANNIE *goes disconsolately to the doorway right. In the doorway she collides with* STANLEY, *who is entering.*

Oh, it's you, is it?

STANLEY I saw you pass my compartment. Thought I'd come along and join you.

JEANNIE I'm just away.

STANLEY Why?

JEANNIE The man says I'll need to wait.

STANLEY What for?

JEANNIE The second service.

STANLEY Rubbish!

JEANNIE All the seats for the first are reserved.

STANLEY *(jangling some coins in his trouser-pocket)* Soon fix that up. Hi, there!

The ATTENDANT *comes forward.*

ATTENDANT M'sieu?

STANLEY A table for two for the first service, please. *(He slips a coin into the* ATTENDANT's *hand)*

ATTENDANT *(accepting the coin)* Thank you, m'sieu. *(He indicates the table from which* JEANNIE *has been evacuated)* Will this do for m'sieu?

STANLEY Aye, it's champion. *(To* JEANNIE*)* Facing, or back? I think you'd better face. *(To the* ATTENDANT*)* Thanks.

Exit the ATTENDANT. STANLEY *puts* JEANNIE *into the seat right of the table. He puts an attaché-case in the rack. He sits left.*

JEANNIE *(seating herself. Full of admiration)* You're very masterful. Do you always get your own way so easy?

STANLEY *(flattered)* Generally.

JEANNIE How much did you pass him?

STANLEY What did I what?

JEANNIE How much did you give him?

STANLEY Half a crown.

JEANNIE Another half-crown! You're very extravagant.

STANLEY Worth it, when you're travelling. A little extra gives you a lot of extra comfort. Are you hungry?

JEANNIE *(searching in her bag for her purse)* Famished. I've had nothing to eat the whole day.

STANLEY No breakfast?

JEANNIE No. I was too excited.

STANLEY Lunch?

JEANNIE The sea was too shoogly. *(She finds her purse)* I stuck it as long as I could. I thought my last hour had come.

STANLEY Take my advice. Next time you cross the Channel have a good solid meal before you start. Pays either way.

JEANNIE I'll need to remember that. *(She hands him some coins)* Here.

STANLEY What's this?

JEANNIE One-and-threepence.

STANLEY What for?

JEANNIE My share of the tip.

STANLEY Here, put this back in your purse.

JEANNIE No, indeed. I can't let you spend your money on me. I'm a stranger.

STANLEY Now look here, I took the half-crown for the porter because it was your luggage. This time it's my affair. I'd have given it him in any case.

JEANNIE Are you telling me the truth?

STANLEY Cross my heart!

JEANNIE All right then, you'll need to let me pay for my own dinner.

STANLEY We'll argue about that when we've had it!

JEANNIE *(putting away her money)* There'll be no argument about it.

STANLEY *(takes off his overcoat and hangs it on a hook left)* Here, don't you think you'd better take your coat off or you won't feel the benefit.

JEANNIE *(takes off her hat and coat, and puts them on the seat)* Well, isn't this nice? All these wee tables. And the wee red frilly lamp-shades!

ATTENDANT *(appearing with bottles down left)* Aperitif, m'sieu?

STANLEY *(to JEANNIE)* What's yours?

JEANNIE What is it?

STANLEY Something to give you an appetite.

JEANNIE That would be a waste. I've got one already.

STANLEY Anyhow, better not, on an empty stomach.

JEANNIE Mine's empty, all right!

STANLEY No, thank you.

ATTENDANT Oui, m'sieu.

He exits down left.

STANLEY Now what about something to drink with the food? I think champagne's indicated, don't you?

JEANNIE Champagne?

STANLEY Don't you like it?

JEANNIE I never tasted it. There was some at my cousin's wedding. Uch, but I was kept that busy it was all gone before I could turn round. I was awful disappointed.

STANLEY We'll make up for it now.

JEANNIE (*opening her handbag and searching for her purse*) How much is it?

STANLEY Put that bag away.

JEANNIE I'll need to pay my share.

STANLEY Now, look here. You can pay for your share of the food, but the drinks are on me. A man always pays for the drinks.

JEANNIE Are you telling me the truth?

STANLEY Didn't you know that?

JEANNIE Well, I've not had much experience of men, except Father. He wouldn't have paid for anybody's drink.

ATTENDANT (*appearing*) You wish to order, m'sieu?

STANLEY (*taking the wine-list, he turns the pages and glances down the list of champagnes*) Yes—now, let's see.

ATTENDANT Number seventeen is a good wine, m'sieu.

STANLEY (*very British accent*) "Gout Americaine"? Not on your life! What's this? Bollinger dix-neuf-vingt-un. Bring us a bottle of that.

ATTENDANT Bien, m'sieu.

STANLEY Tout-de-suite. Pas après le repas.

ATTENDANT Bien, m'sieu. (*He goes down left*)

JEANNIE (*again full of admiration*) Do you speak French?

STANLEY (*making light of it*) Have to in business. (*He takes off his coat*)

JEANNIE It's not everyone could do it, whether they had to or not. Can you manage German as well?

STANLEY I can.

JEANNIE You must be awful clever! Are you travelling on business just now?

STANLEY As a matter of fact, I'm just on my way to the Vienna Fair.

JEANNIE *(delighted)* Is there a Fair on in Vienna?

STANLEY It's more what we'd call a Trade Exhibition.

JEANNIE *(a little dashed)* Well, what are you exhibiting?

STANLEY Just a little invention of my own.

JEANNIE *(awed)* Are you an inventor, too?

STANLEY Only in a small way, you know.

JEANNIE *(short pause)* Are you not going to tell me what it is?

STANLEY Something very ordinary and common.

JEANNIE What?

STANLEY A simplified washing-machine.

JEANNIE *(thrilled)* A washing-machine? Do you mean for clothes?

STANLEY Aye.

JEANNIE Does it take sheets?

STANLEY It does.

JEANNIE *(gazing at him with wonder)* You call that ordinary and common? I don't. It's what I've been wanting all my life.

STANLEY *(pleased)* Is it? I hope other ladies feel the same.

JEANNIE They will, if they have the washing to do. What made you think of it?

STANLEY When I was a kid I used to see my mother bending over the wash-tub. It was back-breaking work.

JEANNIE No one knows that better than me. Can I get seeing it?

STANLEY Aye, if you come to the Fair.

JEANNIE I'll do that all right. When's it on?

STANLEY Opens next Sunday.

JEANNIE Sunday? Do they open a Fair on a Sunday?

STANLEY They do.

JEANNIE What would Father have said?

STANLEY *(amused)* I don't know, I'm sure.

JEANNIE *(throwing* FATHER *overboard once and for all)* Sunday or no Sunday, I'll be there the first day. I'll not rest till I see that washing-machine.

STANLEY I like your enthusiasm.

JEANNIE If you'd washed as many sheets as I have, you'd be enthusiastic too.

STANLEY D'you mean to tell me a little lady like you has had to wash sheets?

JEANNIE Aye. And done everything else in the house as well.

STANLEY *(his turn to admire)* That's very sporting of you.

JEANNIE I didn't do it for sport. Father wouldn't have anyone in. He made out he couldn't afford it. Then if he didn't go and leave two hundred pounds!

STANLEY *(tries to seem impressed)* Two hundred pounds?

JEANNIE Aye. Not counting the funeral. He paid into a Society for that. You could have knocked me down. *(A pause)* I'm spending it on a holiday.

STANLEY All of it?

JEANNIE All except a wee bit I've put by in the bank to keep me going till I find a situation. My cousins in Glasgow wanted me to live with them, turn about. But I'd liefer be independent.

STANLEY Aye, there's nothing like independence. What sort of situation?

JEANNIE A housekeeper.

STANLEY Will you like that?

JEANNIE Fine! You can ask a pound a week and an evening off and every second Sunday and a whole day a month. And I can refuse to wash sheets. As I said to Mistress Whitelaw, it sounds like Paradise.

STANLEY Who's Mistress Whitelaw?

JEANNIE My neighbour. Angus Whitelaw married her on last July. He met her at a place called Southend. Father said it served him right for taking his holiday in England, but I get on with her fine.

STANLEY You'd get on with anyone.

JEANNIE I can hold my own.

STANLEY *hides his amusement. A short silence.*

(*feeling the need to account for her extravagance*) I've never had a holiday except a wee jaunt down the Clyde. Now I want to see the world so's I'll have something to look back on in my old age.

STANLEY Your old age? That's a long way off.

JEANNIE Not so long as all that. Time slips by without you noticing it. How old d'you think I am?

STANLEY Do you want the truth?

JEANNIE Aye, I'm a stickler for the truth.

STANLEY I warn you... I pride myself on guessing people's ages!

JEANNIE Go ahead.

STANLEY Now, let me see—er— (*A short pause while he looks at her*)

JEANNIE Uch, don't stare at me so hard. It's awful embarrassing.

STANLEY *(to himself)* Let's see now. Twenty— *(He hesitates, then makes up his mind)* —six. Twenty-six.

JEANNIE Fancy that!

STANLEY *(delighted)* Was I right the first time?

JEANNIE *(avoiding the lie direct)* Some people think I look more.

STANLEY In some ways you look less. You've got young eyes.

JEANNIE *(pleased)* That's because I've led such a pure life.

STANLEY *hides a smile.*

If it's not a rude question, how old are you?

STANLEY Forty-one.

JEANNIE Just right.

STANLEY What for?

JEANNIE *(hastily)* For a man. Are you married?

STANLEY Widower.

JEANNIE Oh, I'm sorry. I shouldn't have asked.

STANLEY I don't usually speak about it. Somehow it's different with you.

JEANNIE Any children?

STANLEY Two lads—both abroad.

JEANNIE It must be awful lonely for you.

STANLEY It is sometimes. I've stuck it for about seven years.

JEANNIE D'you never think of marrying again?

STANLEY That's the danger.

JEANNIE Danger? Why?

STANLEY I've got to the age when I fancy the wrong sort.

JEANNIE What sort?

STANLEY Blondes.

JEANNIE *(a concession)* Some blondes are quite nice.

STANLEY Not for a tired business man. All right for an evening's amusement.

JEANNIE How have you managed to escape?

STANLEY Easy enough. I'm no Clark Gable. You can see that for yourself.

JEANNIE You look kind. That's the main thing.

STANLEY You're wrong there. Most girls prefer a bully.

JEANNIE They should have had Father!

STANLEY Was he a bully?

JEANNIE He's dead. We'll leave it at that.

STANLEY *(after a short pause)* What hotel are you staying at in Vienna?

JEANNIE It's not a hotel. It's what they call a pension. They gave me the name and address at the Perth office.

STANLEY Know your way about?

JEANNIE No. It's my first time.

STANLEY My name's Stanley Smith, and I'm staying at the Splendide. Spelt S-P-L-E-N-D-I-D-E. If you want any help.

JEANNIE Thank you very much, but I hope I'll not require to avail myself. I don't want to be a nuisance to you.

Enter the ATTENDANT, *down left of the table, with champagne.*

(excitedly) Here's the champagne! What a big bottle! Do you think we can manage it?

STANLEY We can have a good try.

ATTENDANT *(presenting the bottle for inspection)* M'sieu?

STANLEY Has it been on the ice?

ATTENDANT Mais oui, m'sieu.

STANLEY *(feels the bottle)* That's all right.

ATTENDANT You wish it open now, m'sieu?

STANLEY Go ahead. Oui. Ouvert.

ATTENDANT Bien, m'sieu. *(He starts to open the bottle left centre)*

JEANNIE I'm that excited!

VOICES *(offstage)* Diner. Premier service. Diner. Premier service. *(A sound of a bell. It becomes fainter and fainter)*

JEANNIE There's the bell. What's he calling out?

STANLEY Dinner. First service.

JEANNIE Does that mean we can start?

STANLEY In a few minutes.

JEANNIE Not before it's time. I feel as if my back's coming through my front. I take mine in the middle of the day.

STANLEY So do I, it's much more sensible.

The ATTENDANT *has now opened the champagne. He pours some into* STANLEY's *glass and spills some.*

JEANNIE *(to the* ATTENDANT *left)* Oh, my, there's some on the clean tablecloth!

ATTENDANT Pardon, madame.

STANLEY *(dipping his finger in it and reaching out)* Put it behind your ear. For luck. *(He dabs it behind her ears)*

JEANNIE Is that what they do? Here's some for you too. *(She dabs his ears too)*

They smile at each other.

ATTENDANT *(having poured a small quantity of champagne into* STANLEY's *glass)* M'sieu? *(He waits for* STANLEY *to taste it and pass judgment)*

STANLEY *(tasting it)* That's all right. Remplis.

ATTENDANT (*fills* JEANNIE'*s glass and then* STANLEY'*s. Placing the bottle in its holder; bowing*) M'sieu!

He goes off left.

STANLEY (*raising his glass*) Here's to you. May you have a wonderful holiday.

JEANNIE (*raising her glass*) Thanks. Here's to the success of your washing-machine.

STANLEY Thanks. Make a lot of difference to me if it catches on. I'll be able to slack off a bit.

JEANNIE (*giggling*) Then you can marry a blonde.

STANLEY (*amused*) As you say, I can marry a blonde.

JEANNIE I'm that thirsty! (*She drinks the champagne as if it were lemonade*)

STANLEY Here, here! (*He half rises to prevent her drinking too much*)

Curtain.

ACT II

Scene One

*SCENE—Caisse of the Hotel Splendide, Vienna.
When the curtain rises we get a sense of movement. A*
CLERK *is discovered at the Caisse. An old* **GENTLEMAN**
comes from up left and bids good-bye to the **CLERK.** *The*
WAITER *comes from up left to left centre. A* **PAGE** *comes
from up right.*

FIRST PAGE *(lazily)* Vier und siebzig. Vier und siebzig.

The **WAITER** *signals to the* **FIRST PAGE** *to shout with
more vigour. The* **FIRST PAGE** *straightens himself up
and continues to off left, shouting.*

Vier und siebzig. Vier und siebzig.

A **SECOND PAGE** *comes from up left with two suitcases
belonging to the old* **GENTLEMAN,** *who shakes hands
with the* **CLERK,** *bows to the* **WAITER** *and follows the
old* **GENTLEMAN** *with the two cases to off down right.
An* **AMERICAN WOMAN** *is heard off stage right, who is
talking to a* **SECOND AMERICAN WOMAN.**

AMERICAN WOMAN *(offstage)* Gee, Blanche, get a move on,
I'm tired. I suppose we gotta have something to tell 'em
when we get back home, but standing around listening to
all—

She now enters, being led by another silent **AMERICAN
WOMAN.**

—that bolony about the past sure gets me down. As for looking at all those old monuments! What I want's a noo neck and a noo pair of feet. Who said a highball? *(To the* WAITER) Say, you there, bring a couple of highballs up to Number Seven fast as you know how.

The WAITER *exits up right. They go off left centre.*

(offstage) Where's that elevator? It was here yesterday

FIRST PAGE *(offstage)* Vier und siebzig. Vier und siebzig.

Entering and crossing from left to off right.

Vier und siebzig. Vier und siebzig.

JEANNIE *enters from down right, preceded by a* PAGE *carrying her holdall and pilgrim basket—who leads her to the reception* CLERK.

SECOND PAGE *(indicating the Caisse)* Hier, gnädige Frau.

JEANNIE Thank you, thank you very much.

The SECOND PAGE *bows and waits, hoping for a tip.* JEANNIE, *round to the* CLERK, *rather lost. The* SECOND PAGE *looks her up and down with covert amusement and exits up right.*

CLERK *(right)* Gnädige Frau?

JEANNIE *(left)* Can you speak English?

CLERK Of course.

JEANNIE No "of course" about it. Where I've just come from they couldn't understand a word. How much do you charge?

CLERK For what, madame?

JEANNIE For staying here.

CLERK Single or double room?

JEANNIE Single, of course.

CLERK From fourteen Austrian shillings, madame.

JEANNIE Fourteen Austrian shillings. Wait a minute till I do some arithmetic. *(A pause)* That'll be ten-and-six. It's dearer than I meant. What do you get in for it?

CLERK Please?

JEANNIE Does it include tea?

CLERK No, madame.

JEANNIE Supper, then?

CLERK No, madame.

JEANNIE Only breakfast and dinner?

CLERK It is for the room only, madame.

JEANNIE Ten-and-six just for the room? You certainly know how to charge. Is that the cheapest you have?

CLERK Yes, madame.

JEANNIE *(after hesitating—making up her mind)* I'll take a ten-and-sixpenny one, just for the night, till I look round.

CLERK I regret, madame. To-night we have no room.

JEANNIE No room!

The telephone rings.

CLERK Hullo! Hullo! *(He sits, answering the 'phone)*

JEANNIE Are you sure? They told me at the Perth office it would be quite easy.

CLERK *(answering the 'phone)* Ja, Ja. Jawohl, gnädige frau, ein einzel zimmer mit bad. *(To JEANNIE)* On Sunday is the Vienna Fair, madame.

JEANNIE I know that.

CLERK *(answering the 'phone)* Bester dank, gnädige frau, auf wiedersehen. *(He replaces the receiver)*

JEANNIE Can you give me an idea where to go?

CLERK It is the same in all the hotels, madame.

JEANNIE What will I do?

CLERK I regret I can't help you, madame.

A pause.

JEANNIE *(very much worried)* Oh dear, oh dear, oh dear, oh dear! *(A pause. Then she makes up her mind)* I'll just need to bother Mister Smith again. Could you get him for me, please?

CLERK Who, madame?

JEANNIE Mister Smith.

CLERK *(opening a large book)* The gentleman is staying here, madame?

JEANNIE *(anxiously)* Unless he couldn't get in.

CLERK *(consulting the book)* The initial, madame?

JEANNIE "S." It stands for Stanley.

CLERK When did the gentleman arrive?

JEANNIE About an hour ago. We parted at the station. *(Anxiously)* Is he here?

CLERK Yes, madame. *(Having looked in the register)*

JEANNIE *shows relief.*

Your name, madame?

JEANNIE Jeannie McLean. J-E-A-N-N-I-E, M, small c—capital L-E-A-N.

CLERK Thank you, madame. If madame will take a seat? *(He indicates the seat down left)*

JEANNIE *starts to cross.*

AMERICAN WOMAN *(entering from left centre with her American friend)* It's the motivation and the nuance, I said. "My dear,"

I said— *(She bumps into* JEANNIE*)* I beg your pardon— "If the motivation and the nuance don't get together, where are you?"

JEANNIE *follows them to down right with great interest.*

Just no place at all. The trouble with you and me is our motivation and our nuance is all wrong. "If you ask me," I said, "it's about time both of us looked around for somebody whose motivation and nuance was—"

Both exit down right.

The COUNT *enters from left centre, crosses to the* CLERK *at the desk.* JEANNIE *moves over in front of the settee left.*

COUNT *(to the* CLERK*)* Wollens so lieb sein mir 'ein bleistift? Bitte schoen.

CLERK *(handing a pencil to the* COUNT*)* Jawohl, Herr Graf.

COUNT Danke schoen. *(Writing on an envelope)*

Enter a PAGE *with a large box of flowers.*

PAGE *(offstage)* Vierhundert Bitte. Vierhundert Bitte.

Entering from left.

Vierhundert Bitte. Vierhundetr Bitte.

CLERK *(stopping the* PAGE*)* Page—Mr. Stanley Smith, bitte— *(He gives him a message on a slip of paper)*

PAGE *(taking the message)* Vierhundert Bitte. Mr. Stanley Smith.

JEANNIE *follows the* PAGE *to centre.*

Vierhundert Bitte. *(Going off up right)* Mr. Stanley Smith. Vierhundert Bitte. Mr. Stanley Smith.

JEANNIE *crosses to the* CLERK *at the desk, below the* COUNT, *who looks at her with interest and amusement.*

JEANNIE It was that wee laddie took my luggage. Will it be all right?

CLERK Quite safe, madame.

JEANNIE Thank you. I suddenly remembered it. Excuse me for interrupting you. *(She goes back to the seat left)*

COUNT Servus. *(Handing the pencil back to the* **CLERK***)*

The **COUNT** *looks at* **JEANNIE** *again.*

CLERK Danke schoen, Herr Graf.

Presently **STANLEY SMITH**, *accompanied by the* **PAGE**, *appears.*

STANLEY *(offstage)* Where is the lady? *(He comes into sight (up right)*

PAGE Hier, gnädige Herr. *(He indicates* **JEANNIE***)*

STANLEY *(hands him a coin)* Here you are.

PAGE *(bows—smiles, looks at* **JEANNIE***)* Danke, gnädiger Herr. Danke schoen.

He goes off down right.

STANLEY *(to* **JEANNIE**, *who has risen)* Good afternoon.

JEANNIE I'm sorry to trouble you again.

STANLEY No trouble at all.

JEANNIE That pension I went to. They'd no room.

STANLEY Bad luck.

JEANNIE They haven't got one here either.

STANLEY Nonsense! Who said so?

JEANNIE The man at the desk. It's because of the Fair.

A **BLONDE** *enters up right, and comes down to the* **RECEPTION CLERK**, *who lights her cigarette.*

He says they're full up everywhere. What will I do?

STANLEY I'll talk to him.

JEANNIE I only want it for the night till I look round.

STANLEY Have you had any tea?

JEANNIE No.

STANLEY Like some?

JEANNIE I'd give my soul for it.

STANLEY *(amused)* No need for that. Come into the lounge. I'd just ordered some when I heard my number called.

JEANNIE Did I take you away from it?

STANLEY That's all right. I'll enjoy it all the more in your company.

The BLONDE *drops down to the jewel table right, giving sidelong glances at* STANLEY.

JEANNIE There's a girl that looks as if she knows one of us. It can't be me.

STANLEY Where?

JEANNIE Over there. She's a blonde. *(As he looks)* Do you know her?

The BLONDE *smiles at* STANLEY.

STANLEY Never seen her before in my life.

JEANNIE She's smiling at us.

STANLEY *(more casually than he need)* Must be at someone else. Come on. This way.

STANLEY *takes* JEANNIE'*s left arm and swings her round up stage centre.*

JEANNIE What about my room?

STANLEY I'll see about it after tea.

JEANNIE Will that not be too late?

Both moving slowly up stage. The **BLONDE** *crosses to where they had been sitting. She sits down stage on the arm of the settee, concealing* **JEANNIE**'s *umbrella, which she has forgotten.*

STANLEY Don't worry. I'll see you get one. Trust me.

JEANNIE *(relaxes)* Somehow I feel I can. *(She stops and turns)* Oh, my umbrella!

STANLEY *(goes to get it. To the* **BLONDE***)* Excuse me. *(He gets the umbrella, then goes back to* **JEANNIE***)*

JEANNIE Your Blonde's still smiling at us.

Exit **JEANNIE** *and* **STANLEY** *up right. The* **BLONDE,** *who has risen to allow* **STANLEY** *to get the umbrella, smiles after* **STANLEY** *and sits—smiling at the* **CLERK,** *who smiles back.*

Curtain.

Scene Two

*SCENE—Part of a smaller lounge leading to the main
lounge of the Hotel Splendide, Vienna. Anyone sitting
in the smaller lounge can see through to the main one.
We need not do so, but we must get an impression of
grandeur. There is a double writing-desk with concealed
lighting on the low partition between the two parts—a
table with newspapers—and a small low table set for
tea. The sound of an unseen orchestra.*

When the curtain rises, a WAITER *enters up right.*
STANLEY *and* JEANNIE *follow.*

STANLEY Is this the best table you've got?

WAITER I regret there is no room in the big lounge, gnädiger
Herr.

STANLEY Oh, well, it's nicely out of the draught. Is it all right
for you? Would you like to sit there?

The WAITER *shows* JEANNIE *into the chair left of the
table, then moves to centre of the table.*

Thank you.

The WAITER *exits up right.*

JEANNIE *(sits—stares off)* My, what a big room! Isn't it
wonderful? Look at yon ceiling. All that gold!

STANLEY Aye, not so bad. *(He sits right of the table)*

JEANNIE And music. I like this fine.

STANLEY You like everything.

JEANNIE It's all new to me. That's why.

The WAITER *enters from up right and goes towards the
door right.*

STANLEY Certainly nothing blasé about you.

JEANNIE Nothing what?

STANLEY It's very refreshing to be with someone so easily pleased. *(He raises his voice)* Herr Ober!

WAITER Bitteshön, mein Herr? *(He drops right of* STANLEY*)*

STANLEY Noch einen tee, bitte.

WAITER Jawohl, mein Herr.

STANLEY While you're at it you might as well bring another cup and saucer.

WAITER Jawohl.

STANLEY Sofort, bitte.

WAITER Gewiss.

The WAITER *goes off up right.*

JEANNIE *(who has been listening with admiration)* You can make light of it, but it's awful clever of you, being able to speak and understand different languages. At that pension I fairly got tired out, trying to make them understand.

STANLEY *(flattered)* You need your tea, then? Get on with it. Don't wait for me.

The WAITER *enters up right with a cup, saucer and plate on a tray.*

JEANNIE I'll pour this for you.

STANLEY Keep it yourself.

JEANNIE *(stirs the tea in the pot)* Here's the other cup, anyhow. We'll not require to quarrel about it.

WAITER *(places the cup, etc., on the table)* Bitte schön.

JEANNIE *(smiles at him)* Thanks. You've been very quick. Where's the cosy?

WAITER Pardon, madame?

JEANNIE You've forgotten the cosy. *(To* STANLEY*)* How would you say "cosy"?

STANLEY You won't get any cosy here.

JEANNIE No cosy? *(Making a little derisive Scottish noise that can't be spelt)* I'll just need to get used to their ways. *(She pours the tea)*

STANLEY *(to the* WAITER*)* That's all right.

WAITER Danke schön, mein Herr. *(He bows—goes off up right)*

JEANNIE Three lumps. *(She puts them in)*

STANLEY Fancy you remembering that!

JEANNIE Of course I remember. *(She hands him a cup and saucer)* I'll remember the meals I had with you in the train all my life.

STANLEY *(takes the cup and saucer)* Even in your old age?

JEANNIE Aye. *(She pours her own tea)* Even in my old age. But I don't want to think of that now. I keep on wondering what Mistress Whitelaw would say.

STANLEY Why Mistress Whitelaw especially?

JEANNIE She was always on at me to enjoy myself.

STANLEY Wise woman.

JEANNIE She didn't look on me as if I was finished.

STANLEY Finished?

JEANNIE Lots of people think you should be at my age.

STANLEY At twenty-six?

JEANNIE *(remembers that she is thirty-one)* Is your tea all right?

STANLEY Fine, thanks. *(A pause)* Are you finished?

JEANNIE I haven't begun yet. *(She drinks)*

STANLEY I meant with life.

Enter the **BLONDE** *from down right, carrying a sheet of notepaper. She crosses to the writing-table and takes an envelope.*

JEANNIE So did I. There's yon Blonde again.

The **BLONDE** *puts a letter in the envelope and seals it.*

STANLEY *(uses his will-power to keep his eyes from temptation—indicates plates on the table)* Cake or sandwich?

JEANNIE I'm not hungry. I'll just take a cake.

STANLEY *(gazes at them intently)* Which one?

Exit the **BLONDE** *up right.*

JEANNIE That one there. It looks the most indigestible. *(She takes it)* What about you?

STANLEY No, thanks. Mind if I smoke?

JEANNIE Go ahead.

A short pause while she eats and drinks, and he lights a cigarette.

Quite domestic, aren't we?

STANLEY *(looks at her with a smile)* Quite. It's a long time since I've felt like this.

Another short pause.

JEANNIE More tea?

STANLEY *(passes a cup and saucer)* I don't mind if I do. Add a bit to that, will you?

JEANNIE *(takes the cup and saucer)* Not so bad, is it, considering? *(She pours tea)*

STANLEY No, it's all right. What are you doing this evening?

JEANNIE I haven't thought about it yet.

STANLEY Would you like to go round the town in an open carriage? See the sights. End up for a bite of food in one of the big cafés?

JEANNIE Do you mean it?

STANLEY Of course. What d'you think?

JEANNIE It sounds too good to be true. Can you spare the time?

STANLEY Yes. I'm free the whole evening. Don't start work till to-morrow.

JEANNIE I don't know how to thank you.

STANLEY Don't try.

JEANNIE Why are you so kind to me?

STANLEY Don't put it like that, please.

A short pause. JEANNIE *drinks tea.*

Why have the men let you stay single?

JEANNIE Because they have bad taste.

STANLEY *(amused)* That's what I think. *(He puts his cup on the table)*

JEANNIE I never got going out and about. First I was my mother's companion. I liked that fine. While she was alive I never wanted anyone else. She needed me, too. She'd a thin time with father. When I think of him having all that money put by and her having to scrape and save! She never had anything. He never even gave her a civil word.

STANLEY Why didn't she leave him?

JEANNIE She liked him.

STANLEY I suppose you mean she was in love with him?

JEANNIE I suppose I do mean that. *(A short pause)* Life's awful funny when you think of it.

STANLEY And the funniest part of it all is sex.

JEANNIE *(drawing herself up)* We never speak about sex in Scotland, Mr. Smith.

STANLEY I beg your pardon. My mistake.

A short pause. STANLEY SMITH *hides a smile.*

JEANNIE Mother made me promise never to leave him.

STANLEY That wasn't fair.

Enter the BLONDE *up right. She crosses down, catching* STANLEY's *eye.*

JEANNIE Sometimes I think that myself. Time passes so quick. You wake up and find you've missed everything.

Exit the BLONDE *down right.*

Do you think you know her after all?

STANLEY Who?

JEANNIE Yon Blonde.

STANLEY Now, look here—I don't know her and she doesn't know me. *(He rises to avoid further discussion)* I'll go now and see about your room. Better get it settled up. *(He takes a paper from his pocket)* Here's yesterday's "Daily Mail." *(He puts it on the table)*

JEANNIE *(stiffly)* Thank you.

STANLEY *(ashamed of himself)* Sorry.

JEANNIE It's my own fault for being so inquisitive.

STANLEY I'd no call to speak to you like that.

JEANNIE I'm quite used to it.

STANLEY That's a nasty one!

JEANNIE I meant it to be.

STANLEY Come on, now. Be friends.

JEANNIE I am friends.

STANLEY Then give me one of your nice smiles. *(Behind the table, right of* **JEANNIE***)*

JEANNIE *(smiles at him)* You'd get round a lamp-post.

STANLEY *(relieved)* That's better. Have a cigarette?

JEANNIE I told you before—I don't know how to smoke.

STANLEY I was only teasing. *(He leaves the packet on the table)*

JEANNIE Get away with you!

STANLEY Bye-bye.

JEANNIE Bye-bye. If you can't be good, be careful.

STANLEY I'm always that.

JEANNIE That's what I answered when my cousin said it to me.

STANLEY Well? Aren't you?

JEANNIE Not so very. I'm speaking to you.

STANLEY One thing I'll say about you—you can hold your own.

JEANNIE I told you that the first day we met.

STANLEY Bye-bye again.

JEANNIE Bye-bye.

> **STANLEY** *goes off up right. The* **COUNT** *enters up right.*

COUNT Pardon, madame?

> **JEANNIE,** *surprised, looks at him. She sees a slim, carefully dressed, really aristocratic-looking man of about fifty.*

JEANNIE Yes? What is it?

COUNT Has madame finished with the English newspaper?

JEANNIE I haven't started it yet.

COUNT *(bows)* Oh! I am so sorry. Excuse me. *(He moves towards the exit down stage right)*

JEANNIE *(relents)* Go on. Take it. I don't want it.

COUNT *(bows again)* I thank you. *(A short pause)* It is permitted that I sit at this table?

JEANNIE So far as I'm concerned, you can.

COUNT *(sits right of the table)* Thank you very much. The lounge is very full to-day. One has difficulty in finding a place.

JEANNIE It's because of the Fair.

COUNT Yes, of course—because of the Fair.

A pause.

JEANNIE Excuse me for mentioning it—you speak English very well. If it's not a rude question, where did you learn?

COUNT When I was a child I had an English governess.

JEANNIE That accounts for it. I wish I could speak languages.

COUNT It is not necessary. With English one can go anywhere.

JEANNIE So they made out at the Perth office. It's not true. I tried to get a room where they couldn't understand a word. It was awful awkward. I began to get alarmed.

The **WAITER** *appears right with a teapot and hot water.*

That's why I came here.

COUNT Madame is a stranger to my country?

JEANNIE I've only just come... What's this for?

WAITER The second tea, madame.

JEANNIE We've had all we needed.

WAITER *(troubled)* It has been ordered, madame.

JEANNIE That's all right. Just put it down.

WAITER *(relieved)* Thank you, madame. *(He takes the used teapot and hot-water jug and places fresh tea, etc., on the table)*

JEANNIE *(to the* **COUNT***)* Have you had your tea?

COUNT Not yet, madame.

JEANNIE Could you take a cup? It's a pity to waste it.

COUNT *(bows with dignity)* Thank you.

JEANNIE *(to the* WAITER*)* Just bring another cup and saucer.

WAITER Yes, madame. *(He goes off up right)*

COUNT You have not yet seen Wien? Vienna?

JEANNIE Only from the taxi window. I'm going round the town to-night with Mister Smith the man I was with just now. I met him on the journey. He's awful kind.

COUNT Kindness is much in these so hard days, madame.

JEANNIE That's what I think. I'd sooner have a kind man than a handsome one. He looked after my luggage and got me a sleeper and saw that I had my meals. Mind you, I settled up with him. I insisted on that. I hate a sponger.

COUNT A what, madame?

JEANNIE A sponger. Someone that lets the other body pay for everything. I let him stand the champagne. He says a man always pays for the drinks. I must say I was relieved. It was awful dear.

Enter the WAITER *up right.*

(she smiles at remembered pleasure) My, but it was good. I know now why people drink. *(As the* WAITER *brings a cup and saucer)* Thank you.

The WAITER *removes the used cups and saucers—places fresh ones.* JEANNIE *holds out her hand.*

Give me back my cup, please. I'll take a wee thing more to keep this gentleman company.

The WAITER *does so.*

Thanks.

The WAITER *bows—answers her smile and goes off right.*

(to the COUNT*)* How many lumps?

COUNT No milk—no sugar.

JEANNIE *(pouring tea)* No sugar and milk in your tea?

COUNT If you please, madame.

JEANNIE Fancy! It looks more like medicine. *(Hands cup and saucer to the* COUNT*)*

COUNT *(takes cup and saucer)* To each country his taste.

JEANNIE They told me at the Perth office not to be surprised at anything. *(She offers cakes)* Help yourself.

COUNT Thank you.

He takes two with cake-tongs. She watches him with awe, then as he starts to eat them with a fork, she takes one herself—also with tongs, but awkwardly. She eats with a fork and is pleased with her success.

Madame travels alone?

JEANNIE Aye.

COUNT I beg your pardon.

JEANNIE Yes.

COUNT It is not agreeable for a lady to travel alone.

JEANNIE It's better than not travelling at all.

COUNT Madame has taste for adventure? *(He eats and drinks)*

JEANNIE This is my first chance. My father died a few weeks ago and left me his fortune.

The COUNT *turns to her with deep interest.*

I'm taking a wee holiday before settling down. Vienna's my first choice.

COUNT *(bows)* I am honoured.

JEANNIE Are you a native?

COUNT I beg your pardon.

JEANNIE You were born in Vienna?

COUNT Alas, yes.

JEANNIE Why "alas"?

COUNT For a man to have been born in Vienna is to have seen much that is sad.

JEANNIE You could say that about anywhere.

COUNT More of Vienna than of another place, madame. I speak as one who knows. Vienna has been the gayest, the most cosmopolitan city of the world. How could it be otherwise? The Viennese have the—how does one say? —the genius for to be gay—for to smile—for to sing—for to dance. When one is *persona grata* at the Court as my family has been, one has everything. Now we have no more a Court—no more a country, no more the light heart. No more do we dance and sing. *(He pulls himself back)* Forgive that I speak of this thing.

JEANNIE *(enthralled)* Go on. I'm interested.

COUNT One must not spoil your holiday.

JEANNIE It's all part of it. I mean I like to hear everything.

COUNT *(brings from his pocket a shabby but good card-case)* My card, madame. *(He hands it to her)* Count Karl.

JEANNIE *(reads—excited)* Are you a Count? A real one?

COUNT Yes, madame.

JEANNIE A real one.

COUNT Yes, madame.

JEANNIE Fancy that! I'll need to write and tell my cousins. They'll be awful jealous. I can crow over Colin's stuck-up relations. I'll need to let Mistress Whitelaw know too. *(With sudden excitement)* Do you hear what they're playing?

The music swells.

"The Blue Danube." *(She lowers her voice to meet the occasion)* The very thing I came for. And I'm hearing it the first day. *(Moved)* At last! I've got something I wanted at last. I'm hearing "The Blue Danube" played at the source. My, that's nice. Do you mind if we keep quiet while we listen to it? ...

The music swells. The COUNT *shakes his head in negation. Hands cigarettes.* JEANNIE *shakes her head in negation, but signs to him to smoke. He prepares to do so, then seeing her ecstatic expression, refrains from striking a match. The* COUNT, *half touched, half amused, watches her.*

STANLEY SMITH *enters, unnoticed, from up right, comes to between the* COUNT *and* JEANNIE.

The music fades down a little.

STANLEY Sorry to have kept you waiting so long.

JEANNIE *(startled)* Has it been long? I didn't notice. I've been talking to this gentleman.

COUNT *(rises—bows)* Excuse.

STANLEY *(to the* COUNT*)* That's all right. Don't move. We're just going.

COUNT I thank you. There is now a vacant place in the great lounge. *(He bows to* JEANNIE*)* Good day, madame. I thank you for your hospitality.

JEANNIE That's all right. I've enjoyed your company. I hope I see you again.

COUNT Madame, I am at your service. *(He bows)* Madame, m'sieu. *(Bows to* STANLEY. *He moves to the exit down right, turns to* JEANNIE—*bows and says:)* Madame.

JEANNIE *gives a tiny wave of her hand and the* COUNT *exits down right.*

STANLEY *(brusquely)* Who's your friend?

JEANNIE *(proudly)* He's a Count.

STANLEY Who told you?

JEANNIE *(her smile fades)* He did. Here's his card. It's all right. Anyone can see at a glance he's an aristocrat.

STANLEY *(reads the card and drops it on the table)* Well, I... I don't want to interfere, but you have to be a bit careful who you pick up.

JEANNIE *(indignant)* Mister Smith, I'll thank you not to talk to me like that. I don't pick people up. But I'm polite enough to answer when they speak to me.

STANLEY Did you invite him to sit at this table?

JEANNIE No, I didn't. He asked my permission to take a seat because there wasn't one anywhere else.

STANLEY *(unpleasantly)* There wasn't one here. *(He sees the empty plates)* Hello? Someone's been having a pretty good tea at my expense.

JEANNIE At my expense—I'll pay for it myself. I didn't think you were so mean. How much do I owe you? *(Opening her bag)*

STANLEY Put that bag away.

JEANNIE I insist—if you don't tell me I'll require to ask the waiter.

STANLEY *(raises his voice)* Herr Ober! *(He waits, goes towards the great lounge up right)* Herr Ober!

Enter the WAITER.

WAITER Ein moment. *(He appears up right)* Gnädiger Herr?

STANLEY Wie fiel? *(He moves slightly down stage right)*

WAITER *(troubled by his tone)* Bitte schoen. *(He takes out a pad and pencil and starts to reckon up)* Tea-dessert, Backereien— sandwiches—das macht zwei tee-dreisechszig. Dessert

Bachereien das Stuck siep zig zwei achtzig. Sandwiches—
drei dreissig—Das macht also acht siepzig—noch zehn per
cent im Gauzen neun schilling sechzig Groschen ich bin
so frei. *(He starts to clear the table and pick up the tray;
leaves the packet of cigarettes on the table, and the "Daily
Mail".)*

JEANNIE *can't believe her ears.*

STANLEY *(takes the money from his purse and gives it to the
WAITER)* That's all right.

WAITER *(bows and smiles)* Danke, gnädiger Herr. Danke sehr.
(He bows—goes off right)

JEANNIE How much is my share? Including the Count.

STANLEY *(annoyed)* Very well, then. Knocking off my pot of
tea, that leaves— *(Does speedy arithmetic)* —seven-and-six.

JEANNIE *(hiding her dismay)* And my share of the tip?

STANLEY If you must be exact. Eight-and-thripence.

JEANNIE *(hands him a note)* Here's a ten-shilling note. Will
you give me the right change, please.

STANLEY *(looks at her, counts out the change)* Stubborn little
thing!

JEANNIE If I keep my independence I won't require to put up
with any impertinence. *(She takes the change)* What about
my room? Did you manage to get one?

STANLEY Yes, I did. It's one of their best with a bathroom.

JEANNIE A bathroom! How much is it?

STANLEY They're letting you have it for the same price as a
cheaper one.

JEANNIE Why?

STANLEY I talked to them. Would you like to go and have a
look at it?

JEANNIE Where is it?

STANLEY The Reception Manager'll show you up.

The WAITER *enters, crosses right to left.*

I'll take you to him. *(He calls)* Herr Ober!

WAITER Bitteschön?

STANLEY I'll be back in a minute. Don't let anyone else take this table.

WAITER Very good, sir.

He exits up left.

JEANNIE *(as they go)* Do you mean I have a bathroom all to myself?

STANLEY Yes.

JEANNIE Can I get taking a bath whenever I like?

STANLEY Yes.

JEANNIE Wonders never cease! *(Exit)*

The music now plays. The WAITER *enters from up left, moves to the table left and tidies it. A* PAGE *enters from down right with an ashpan and goes to the table down right and empties the ashtray. The* WAITER *"hisses" to the* PAGE *to clear the ashtrays at the table left centre; he does so. The* WAITER *"hisses," he empties same ashtray again. The* WAITER *"hisses" again, points to the table down left. The* PAGE *crosses to it, empties the ashtray but keeps a half-smoked cigarette, looks at the* WAITER, *sees he is looking and empties the ashtray again. The* PAGE *then goes up left and exits. The* WAITER *places "Reserved" card on the table left centre and exits up left.*

At the WAITER's *third hiss to the* PAGE *the* BLONDE *enters from up right, strolls down stage right and then over to the table left centre, takes up "reserved" card, places it upside-down, sits on the chair left, takes a cigarette out of the packet left by* STANLEY, *lights it, when* STANLEY SMITH *re-enters. He looks with surprise at the* BLONDE, *recognizes her, makes it clear that he isn't too pleased—is above table where she sits, right of her chair.*

STANLEY Good afternoon.

BLONDE *(unabashed by his tone)* Good afternoon.

STANLEY You speak English, do you?

BLONDE Of course.

STANLEY Then you'll understand me when I tell you that this table's engaged.

BLONDE *(without moving)* So?

STANLEY *(firmly)* Sorry. *(He waits)* P'raps you'll be kind enough to go back to your own?

BLONDE That is not possible. Already it is occupied.

STANLEY I'll call the waiter to find you another.

BLONDE *(still seated)* The gnädiger Heer is polite.

STANLEY No, he's not. He's from Yorkshire.

BLONDE Please?

STANLEY *(worried)* Come on. The lady'll be back in a minute.

BLONDE The lady?

STANLEY Don't pretend you don't know who I mean. *(Behind the table left centre)*

BLONDE She is the Heer's wife?

STANLEY No. Anyhow, it's no business of yours. Oh, come on!

BLONDE *(giving in gracefully—rises and crosses to settee right)* I make a mistake. I think, by the way he look at me, the Heer is interested?

STANLEY Sorry. I'll pay you the compliment of telling you you're the sort of girl any man'd have to look at twice. *(Behind the table)*

BLONDE *(pleasantly)* I give the Heer also a compliment. *(She crosses to* STANLEY *and leans over the chair right of the table left centre)* When I see him I say me— "There is a man. At last there is a man. How nice shall it be to speak with him—to have a dinner—a cabaret. To show him a little the life of Vienna before a so hard week at the Fair."

STANLEY How d'you know I'm here for the Fair?

BLONDE For what else shall come a man such as the Heer to Vienna? Not for to waste his time in amusement. He is too serious—no?

STANLEY *(on his mettle)* I'm serious about my work. But I know how to enjoy myself.

BLONDE I also am serious about my work.

STANLEY Your work? *(He smiles cynically)* D'you call this work?

BLONDE Please?

STANLEY Do you call this work? Picking up stray foreigners?

BLONDE *(with dignity)* I'm afraid the Heir becomes a little too polite. I thank him. Guten-tag. *(She crosses up right)*

STANLEY Oh, miss—I'm sorry. It was a natural mistake. In my country pretty girls like you don't do this sort of thing unless—well, unless they do it for a living. I apologize. *(A short pause, moving up to the* BLONDE*)* What was that you were saying about dinner and a cabaret?

BLONDE *(with a little shrug)* It cannot interest the Herr.

STANLEY It does interest me. The trouble is I'm rather busy this evening. What about to-morrow?

BLONDE To-morrow is Saturday. On Saturday after mittagessen go I into the mountains.

STANLEY What about the evening?

BLONDE In the mountains I stay the whole night. And on Sunday all day.

STANLEY Sunday evening, then?

BLONDE Sunday I do not return until very late—only for to go to bed.

STANLEY Monday?

BLONDE On Monday I am again at my work. All the week, while I work, I am too tired to amuse myself.

STANLEY What is your work?

BLONDE I am vendeuse and mannequin in the best atelier in Vienna—it is not so easy. All the day must I stand on my feet. We have much clients. English, American. I must speak with them—smile with them—how do you say it? Persuade them. At night I am tired.

STANLEY If you're so tired, why are you going out to-night?

BLONDE To-morrow is Saturday. I work only for half a day. But it is not important. I waste the Herr's time. Also my own. *(She crosses to the table left, puts out her cigarette)*

STANLEY *(lost)* Damn it all, I must have a bit of fun once in a while! *(To the* BLONDE*)* Er—if I get rid of this appointment you won't let me down, will you?

BLONDE Please? *(A slight move up stage to left of* STANLEY*)*

STANLEY Where shall we meet?

BLONDE Here?

STANLEY Not here. Might be a bit awkward.

BLONDE The Kaiser Bar?

STANLEY Where's that?

BLONDE The Kärtnerstrasse. Five minutes from here.

STANLEY What time?

BLONDE Eight o'clock?

STANLEY Righto. *(Worried)* You won't be annoyed if I ask you to go now? I've got to get rid of this other appointment. It won't do for us to be seen together. Would you mind going to the little Bar—through the lounge there? *(Indicates)*

BLONDE *(crosses to the door right, amused)* I know it!

STANLEY Done it before, have you? *(She smiles assent)* I'll take you as far as the door.

BLONDE I thank you. *(Close to STANLEY)*

STANLEY I'm sorry I can't ask you to have a drink, but I'll make up for it later.

BLONDE *(laughs)* Understood.

They go off down right.

For a few moments we become aware of hotel noises again. The orchestra plays softly a staccato, cynical little piece. JEANNIE reappears up left. Sees empty room— looks anxious, goes uncertainly to the chair, picks up her umbrella and goes out with it. She is just about to disappear when STANLEY returns from the door right.

STANLEY *(enters—smoking a cigarette)* I say, there. Miss McLean?

JEANNIE Oh, I thought you were away. I was just going up to my room.

STANLEY How do you like it?

JEANNIE It's palatial. *(Crossing down centre)* What time do you require me to-night?

STANLEY *(unhappily)* As a matter of fact, I'm afraid I've got a little disappointment for you there.

JEANNIE Oh?

STANLEY I—er—met a business friend just now in the lounge, sort of chap may be very useful to me. The washing-machine, and so on and so forth. To-night's his only free night. Wants to talk shop. Would you be very disappointed if I asked you to postpone our little outing?

JEANNIE D'you mean you want to get out of taking me round the town?

STANLEY Don't put it like that, please. Could you make it another night?

JEANNIE *(tries to hide her intense disappointment)* I'll just need to. Business is business.

STANLEY Are you very disappointed?

JEANNIE It can't be helped.

STANLEY What will you do with yourself?

JEANNIE Uch, I'll just take a bath and get to my bed.

STANLEY Bit dull for you, your first night in Vienna.

JEANNIE I've had enough excitement for one day. If you'll excuse me, I'll away now. *(Moving up stage right)*

STANLEY Have a little drink before you go.

JEANNIE No, thanks.

STANLEY What about your supper?

JEANNIE I've had plenty to eat, thanks. I'll do till tomorrow morning.

STANLEY *(relieved to be out of it so easily, but not relieved of his sense of guilt)* Here's the "Daily Mail." To read in bed. *(He fetches the "Daily Mail" from the table)*

JEANNIE I'll not be reading. I've got too much to think about. Thank you again, for all your kindness. Good night.

STANLEY Good night...

JEANNIE goes up left. He watches her out of sight, throws the paper on the table left centre. Puffs at the cigarette for a moment, then, with an expression of self-disgust, he turns to the ashtray and stubs it out.

You know, Stanley, you're a bit of a rotter.

The orchestra plays as—.

The curtain falls.

Scene Three

SCENE—The same corner of the lounge. Next morning.

When the curtain rises the COUNT *is discovered writing at the desk up centre, on right of it, presumably writing a letter. The* WAITER *enters from down right with two English papers on their holders, and hangs them on the paper-rack down left and then to centre as* JEANNIE *enters without a hat. She seems rather forlorn. She sees the* WAITER *and looks relieved—is now centre and right of him. She carries a picture postcard.*

JEANNIE Good morning.

WAITER Guten morgen, meine gnädigste, kuss die hand, meine gnädigste.

JEANNIE Could you tell me where to write my postcard?

WAITER *(showing her up stage left of the table)* Hier, bitte schön.

JEANNIE Is that a writing-desk? *(Going to the seat as the* WAITER *pulls it out—she sits)*

WAITER Gewiss, meine gnädigste.

JEANNIE Thank you.

WAITER Bitte schön.

He exits up right.

COUNT *(after a pause)* Good morning.

JEANNIE *(startled—smiles on looking up as she recognizes him)* Oh, it's you, is it? Good morning.

COUNT A beautiful day, is it not?

JEANNIE Wonderful. The sun came in first thing at my bedroom window. I just basked in it.

COUNT They give you a comfortable room?

JEANNIE Give is hardly the word. But I must say it's nice. In fact it's luxurious. Mind you, they know how to charge.

COUNT If madame can afford to pay?

JEANNIE I can do that all right. But I don't like being robbed.

COUNT *(rises)* Who does, madame? Did you enjoy the evening?

JEANNIE Well, no, as a matter of fact, Mr. Smith couldn't take me round the town after all. I went out for a walk by myself. It was awful lonely.

COUNT I'm so sorry—a thousand pities! I had been so happy to escort madame.

JEANNIE Do you really mean that?

COUNT Did I not say so yesterday? I am at madame's service.

JEANNIE I thought you were just being polite. Why should you bother?

COUNT *(bows)* I wish for so a charming stranger to my country, that the first impression shall be agreeable.

He leans over the writing-table close to JEANNIE, *who nervously rises and crosses to the exit up right. The* COUNT *makes a movement to stop her.*

Also like I very much to speak again English. By the way— this— *(With the slightest suggestion of disdain)* —Mister Smith, he is your escort to-day?

JEANNIE No. He hasn't the time. He's got to get his stall dressed for the Fair. *(Slightly right of the writing-table)*

COUNT So? *(A short pause)* Madame has arrange for herself a interesting programme?

JEANNIE No, I haven't. That's the trouble. I thought it'd be quite easy, but I feel awful kind of lost on my own. I was just wondering whether to go to Cook's and hire a guide. They advised me to do that at the Perth office. What do you think?

COUNT Madame, don't you wish to accept my offer?

JEANNIE Does it hold good through the day?

COUNT Oh, madame!

JEANNIE What about your work?

COUNT I do not work, madame.

JEANNIE Can you manage without? *(A slight move downstage left)*

COUNT Fortunately I have the rents from my estate.

JEANNIE *(impressed)* You have an estate, have you?

COUNT From my mother. The castle from the family of my father is our property, alas, no more.

JEANNIE That's awful sad.

COUNT Such is life, madame, such is life. But we shall not speak of this to-day. What do you want to see?

JEANNIE Everything.

COUNT But at first?

JEANNIE I don't know. I'll just leave it to you.

COUNT Let me consider. Do please sit down.

He takes her left arm and pilots her to the chair right of the table left centre. She sits, and he moves left of her and sits upstage arm of the chair left of the table.

Ah, yes. First I think the Spanish Riding School where are the white stallions from the Imperial stable. In all the world there are no horses more beautiful. Then perhaps for a little lunch at the "Drei Husaren" —a restaurant which is managed by three officers formerly in the Hussars. In all Vienna there is no restaurant more chic. After this to the little Palace of Schönbrunn, where has lived as a girl Marie Antoinette. *(He rises)* In all the world is no Palace with more charm. Then for to-night? *(He crosses centre)* Ah, yes, to-night. *(Turning to her)* Madame, the admirer of Strauss must go in the Opera. To-night it is a gala—a gala in honour of Strauss—the Strauss which has composed your favourite waltz— "The Blue Danube."

JEANNIE *(her eyes aglow)* "The Blue Danube." Will they be playing it?

COUNT *(moving nearer to JEANNIE)* With full orchestra. All the best people will be there. It shall be gay—amusing. Not alas, as formerly. Then, mein Gott—ah then— *(He steps centre)* it has been a sight one cannot forget. The ladies in their most beautiful gowns—the officers in uniform—the great staircase—the glittering chandeliers—the jewels which sparkle like sunshine on the Mediterranean sea. Madame, if I could bring this picture to your eyes.

JEANNIE *(entranced)* You do.

COUNT *(sadly)* No. It is not possible. One does not feel the life; one does not hear the laughter; one does not breathe again the perfume of a glove on a little hand... *(A pause. He controls his emotion. Presently he speaks again)* Pardon, madame. I mustn't talk about these things. *(He puts out his cigarette in the ashtray on the table down right)*

JEANNIE *(awed)* Please go on.

COUNT For me it is too sad. *(With change of tone)* But positively madame must go to the Opera to-night.

JEANNIE Will you be there?

COUNT No, madame. *(He crosses to centre)*

JEANNIE Do you not want to go?

COUNT I would love to.

JEANNIE Then what's to hinder you?

COUNT I beg your pardon?

JEANNIE Why don't you?

COUNT Because for a few days—a week, perhaps—I must live very quiet.

JEANNIE Why's that?

COUNT A reason of finance.

JEANNIE What a nuisance!

COUNT It is not important. But for the moment I must—as you say in English—go slow.

JEANNIE (*plucks up courage, fingering her handbag*) Would you be offended if I made a suggestion?

COUNT Offended? With you?

JEANNIE (*diffidently*) Would you let me pay for your seat?

COUNT Madame...?

JEANNIE (*troubled*) You are offended. (*She rises*)

COUNT N-no. But I cannot trespass on the generosity of a stranger.

JEANNIE I know just how you feel. I was the same with Mistress Whitelaw and Stanley Smith. But with you it is different. You can return my hospitality when your rents come.

COUNT Madame. Yes, I can return it.

JEANNIE I'd be glad of your company. I don't much like the thought of going on my own. It's the language. Can we get in at the doors?

COUNT I beg your pardon?

JEANNIE Do you require to take tickets in advance?

COUNT But, of course. Already they are not easy to procure. Only the most expensive places remain.

JEANNIE Are they very dear?

COUNT I beg your pardon?

JEANNIE (*opens her handbag*) How much are they?

COUNT I do not know exact. Twenty—twenty-five—thirty shillings.

JEANNIE For the two?

COUNT For one, madame.

JEANNIE *(hides her surprise. Closes her bag)* I'll need to go up to my bedroom and get another traveller's cheque. *(She crosses below the* COUNT *up stage right)* Will you wait a minute?

COUNT I am at madame's service. *(He bows)*

JEANNIE *(pauses, turns)* What do we wear?

COUNT The grande toilette, madame.

JEANNIE What's that?

COUNT Evening dress!

JEANNIE Of course! What a nuisance. I've left mine at home. Could you tell me the name of a shop where I could get one ready-made?

COUNT If madame wish it I escort her to the best atelier.

JEANNIE I'm much obliged. How much will it be?

COUNT One must pay for the best.

JEANNIE *(throws aside her last shred of caution)* Uch, of course. I might as well be killed for a sheep as a lamb. Oh, another thing! Can you tell me where I can buy some powder for my nose?

Quick curtain.

Scene Four

SCENE—The same. The same night. An orchestra is playing off.

When the curtain rises, the WAITER *is discovered at the small table down left. He clears two used lager glasses and two pads on to a tray whilst* STANLEY *enters from up right to right centre. He has had a hard day's work after a late night. He wears his business suit, and goes to settee right and sits.*

WAITER *(left centre)* Wünscht der Herr etwas?

STANLEY I want a pick-me-up. What have you got?

WAITER Eier—Cognac—Martini—Horse's Neck?

STANLEY I'll stick to whisky.

WAITER Whisky-soda?

STANLEY Yes, double-Haig. Quick as you can.

WAITER Bitte schön. *(He crosses to down right)*

STANLEY And bring me the bottle. I like to see what I'm getting.

WAITER Jawohl!

He exits down right.

The COUNT, *in evening dress, enters from up right, crosses to the chair left to retrieve his hat and white gloves which he has presumably left there. As he picks them up the* WAITER *enters from right with a tray on which are whisky and soda and a tumbler.*

(on seeing the COUNT*)* Guten abend, Herr Graf.

COUNT Guten abend, Herr Ober.

He exits up right.

WAITER I'bin so frei! *(He puts the tray on the table right and opens the bottle of soda)*

STANLEY That's all right. Leave the bottle there. I might have another later.

WAITER Bitte schön. *(He crosses to centre)*

STANLEY Herr Ober?

WAITER *(turns)* Bitte schön?

STANLEY Er—that man that was here just now—who is he?

WAITER Wie bitte?

STANLEY That man that calls himself a Count—who is he?

WAITER Ah, yes—the Count.

STANLEY Is he a pukka one?

WAITER Bitte?

STANLEY Is he a real Count?

WAITER Aber—naturlich.

STANLEY I don't know so much about the "naturlich." There's a lot of impostors about.

WAITER *(with respect—a rebuke)* The Count is from one of the best families from Austria, gnädiger Herr.

STANLEY Does he live here?

WAITER In Vienna—yes.

STANLEY I mean does he live in this hotel?

WAITER *(amused)* Aber nein.

STANLEY You mean he can't run to it.

WAITER Bitte?

STANLEY You mean he can't afford it.

WAITER Pardon?

STANLEY Damn it all, man, is he rich or poor?

WAITER Ich weiss nicht! Entschuldigen Sie bitte. *(To escape further examination)* I think I hear a client calls. *(He bows and exits up left)*

STANLEY *(to himself)* Not much change out of him.

> STANLEY *rises and crosses over to the paper-rack, finds "The Times" in its holder and crosses back to the settee right and sits. As he sits, the* BLONDE *enters from up right, looking delightful in holiday clothes.*

BLONDE *(crosses to the table left, puts her stick and bag on it)* Good evening.

STANLEY Good evening. I thought you'd gone to the mountains? *(He places his glass on the table)*

BLONDE Alas, no. I lose my train. *(She crosses to left of STANLEY)*

STANLEY *(sceptical)* How did you manage that?

BLONDE A client. A stupid client who does not come until too late. Positively must have a new evening dress and does not know how to buy. I show to her this one, that one and the other one. This one is too dark, that one is too light, this one is too tight, that one is too plain. Nothing here, too much there. I tell you to-day I work. After so late a night it is not nice. I think!

STANLEY Then I expect after all this fuss, she went out without buying anything?

BLONDE But no. I am not so bad a vendeuse as that. *(She sits left of STANLEY)* But we waste much time. In the end I and the dressmaker also must wait until it is altered for madame. And so I lose the train.

STANLEY Bad luck.

BLONDE *(philosophically)* It is life.

STANLEY Some women ought to be shot. *(He drinks)*

BLONDE I think! *(Mischievous smile)* It was a friend of yours... *(STANLEY looks at her, surprised)* The little lady you were with yesterday. *(STANLEY looks incredulous)* You enjoy yourself last night?

STANLEY Very much, thanks. *(He puts down his glass)*

BLONDE You do not speak with much enthusiasm.

STANLEY I've had a busy day. I'm tired.

BLONDE I also. *(A pause)* You do not ask me to have a little drink?

STANLEY Sorry. To tell you the truth, I'm waiting for someone. A business friend. That's why I didn't ask you to sit down.

BLONDE Pardon me. I get up at once. *(She rises, crosses to fetch her stick from the table left and then back to left centre)*

STANLEY *(rises to centre)* If you like to order yourself a drink at the bar, you can put it down to me.

BLONDE *(mollified)* Many thanks. You wish that I show to you another cabaret to-night?

STANLEY Now run along. *(She crosses him towards the door right)* Get yourself some cigarettes.

BLONDE Thank you.

STANLEY I might be along presently.

BLONDE *(with a touch of irony that is lost on him)* Grüss dich Gott, Schnucher.

She gives a little laugh and exits down right.

STANLEY *to up centre, when the* **WAITER** *enters from up left.*

STANLEY Herr Ober! Herr Ober! Have you seen anything of that little lady this evening?

WAITER This evening, no.

STANLEY Oh well, you might send a page, will you?

WAITER Sofort, gnädiger Herr.

He goes off up right. STANLEY *sits left of the writing-table
and begins to write. The* PAGE *comes in up right from
the hall and stands waiting. He fidgets and scratches
himself.* STANLEY *becomes aware of him.*

STANLEY Stand still, can't you?

The PAGE *stands to attention.* STANLEY *addresses an
envelope, licks the flap and hands it to the* PAGE.

Take this up to Number Twenty-seven. If the lady's there
wait for an answer.

PAGE Jawohl, gnädiger Herr.

STANLEY What are you waiting for?

PAGE *(embarrased)* Nichts, gnädiger Herr. *(He quickly recovers
his pose, grins—turns to go off up left)*

STANLEY *(relents)* Here you are. *(He holds out a coin)*

PAGE *(turns back, takes coin with delight)* Danke. Danke sehr.

STANLEY *(returns his grin)* Hurry up with that answer.

PAGE Sofort, gnädiger Herr. Danke. Danke. *(He goes quickly
off left)*

STANLEY *gets up from the desk and goes back to his
seat right. He pours more soda to his whisky.* JEANNIE,
*feeling very self-conscious in her new evening dress,
comes in, looking for the* COUNT. *She is transformed
and a little frightened. She has entered up right and
crosses to put the cape and evening bag on the chair
right of the table left.*

JEANNIE Are you not going to say good evening to me,
Mr. Smith?

STANLEY *(looks up, sees who it is and stares with admiration
and amazement at the change in her)* Good evening. *(He
half rises)* Oh, it's you, is it?

JEANNIE Do I look nice? *(A slight move to him)*

STANLEY All right.

JEANNIE *(nervously)* I've been to the dressmaker's.

STANLEY I can see that for myself.

JEANNIE Do you approve of my choice?

STANLEY Not bad. What have you done to yourself?

JEANNIE It's my face. Heaven alone knows what they did to it. I've a whole chemist shop up in my bedroom. They forbid me to wash it, but I will.

STANLEY I should hope so.

JEANNIE I'm glad you agree with me. *(She moves a little nearer)* They have some awful dirty ideas.

STANLEY You know, if you asked me your age to-night *(she quickly looks away to hide a sudden remembrance of her lie)* I shouldn't guess you at twenty-six. More like sixteen.

JEANNIE *(quickly)* We'll split the difference. My skin's quite nice where it hasn't been exposed. *(She indicates her shoulder)* That's not "foundation," it's myself.

STANLEY May I say something?

JEANNIE If it's a compliment.

STANLEY It is.

JEANNIE Go ahead.

STANLEY Your nose isn't so bad either.

JEANNIE Oh, thank you. I've always thought it was my best feature. *(Suddenly self-conscious again)* Am I too bare? *(Nearer to STANLEY)*

STANLEY No.

JEANNIE I wanted something more covered up, but the saleswoman wouldn't let me. *(She sits above STANLEY)* She was an awful blether. I gave in for the sake of peace. *(She

looks at him. He looks non-committal. She holds out a foot)
Do you like my shoes?

STANLEY *(terse because he has been reminded of his bad behaviour)* Not so bad.

JEANNIE My stockings are real silk. They don't let you wear much underneath. I feel like a princess.

STANLEY As a matter of fact, I've just sent a page up to your room with a note asking you if you would have a bit of dinner with me to-night? Can you wait a few minutes while I have a wash and brush-up?

JEANNIE Thank you very much, but I'm engaged.

STANLEY *(disappointed)* Why, what are you doing?

JEANNIE I'm going to the Opera.

STANLEY By yourself?

JEANNIE No.

STANLEY Who with?

JEANNIE Yon Count.

STANLEY The one that picked you up last night?

JEANNIE *(with dignity)* Mister Smith, for the second time I'll thank you not to speak to me like that.

STANLEY Have you made any inquiries about him?

JEANNIE No, I didn't need to. I go by my instinct.

STANLEY Sometimes instinct can be wrong.

JEANNIE I know that. I've just had the experience. *(She gets up, makes a slight move towards her cape on the chair, then turns to STANLEY)* I may's well tell you—I saw you last night with yon Blonde. I'll wish you good-bye.

She goes with dignity up stage centre. At the same moment the COUNT comes in again by the door right. He sees her.

COUNT Madame.

JEANNIE *(turns)* Oh, Count, there you are!

COUNT *(with a gesture that signifies amazement and admiration)* Madame!

JEANNIE *(shyly)* Am I all right?

COUNT *(with emotion)* All right? Madame! *(He goes to her, takes her right hand, bows over it and kisses it and looks into her eyes)* Madame is a queen.

JEANNIE *(with a shy little laugh of pleasure)* I thought I was going a bit far when I called myself a princess. Is it time to go?

COUNT Yes. If we wish to hear the Overture.

JEANNIE I want to hear everything. *(She fetches her cape and bag)*

COUNT *(stands aside, bows, waits like a courtier for her to go out)* Madame... *(He takes her cape and puts it round her shoulders)*

JEANNIE, *in spite of herself, sails out like royalty up right. The* COUNT *follows.* STANLEY *is left alone. He sits for a moment with an expression of baffled annoyance. He is fair enough to know it's his own fault. The* PAGE, *carrying the note on a small salver, comes in from the hall, up left.*

PAGE Bitte, gnädiger Herr?

STANLEY What is it?

PAGE The lady is not in the room, gnädiger Herr.

STANLEY *(angrily)* Damn it! I know that.

PAGE The Herr wish it that I call the number in the lounge and in the dining-room?

STANLEY No. *(He takes the note and tears it across viciously)* I don't.

PAGE *(bows)* Danke, gnädiger Herr.

STANLEY *tears the note across again and throws the pieces into the tray.*

STANLEY *(angrily)* Don't "Dank" me.

He exits up right.

Curtain.

Scene Five

*Waltz thirty seconds and into "High Road" —after
previous waltz.*

SCENE—*A week later. Alcove table in a restaurant. It
is set for supper. We must again have a sense of activity
that we do not see. Soft music plays.*

*When the curtain rises, the Maître d'Hotel is putting
finishing touches to the table. Abruptly the music
changes to a Scottish air.*

*The Maître d'Hotel glances off. He smiles and stands
aside—by the chair left of the table.*

JEANNIE, *wearing the same evening dress decorated
with a posy of flowers, appears up right. Before greeting
the Maitre d'Hotel, she turns and acknowledges with a
queenly little bow the tributes of the orchestra. She then
turns with a smile to the Maître d'Hotel. She has been
living in a fairy-tale world and shows it.*

JEANNIE Good evening, Herr Ober.

HERR OBER Good evening, madame. *(Coming forward behind
the table)*

JEANNIE How are you to-night?

HERR OBER *(bows)* I thank you. And madame?

JEANNIE I'm fine, thanks. The Count's just coming. He's paying
the taxi.

HERR OBER Madame has been in the Opera again?

JEANNIE Yes. A thing called Siegfried. *(She sits left)* Quite nice,
but my favourite's still "The Blue Danube."

*The Maître d'Hotel puts her into a chair left of the table
and moves above the table right of* **JEANNIE.**

Here he is.

Enter the COUNT *up right, wearing tails. He smiles with pleasant friendliness.*

COUNT *(right)* Servus Franzl.

HERR OBER *(bows)* Good evening, Herr Graf.

COUNT You keep our table? Good.

HERR OBER *(bows)* Of course, Herr Graf. *(He sets the* COUNT*'s chair right)*

JEANNIE I don't know about you, Count—I'm hungry.

COUNT I also.

We see that he has a flower in his buttonhole.

JEANNIE It's the music. It takes it out of you.

COUNT *(he sits right)* What wish you to eat?

JEANNIE *(left)* I'll just have my usual. Caviare and some of that Chicken Mousse with a Russian Salad and a Peach Melba.

HERR OBER And the Herr Graf?

COUNT For me the same. Also, to finish, a Savoury Maison.

HERR OBER And to drink?

COUNT And to drink—

JEANNIE I feel like champagne again to-night.

COUNT I, also.

JEANNIE Funny how easy it becomes a habit.

COUNT As with all good things. *(To the Maître d'Hotel)* The same as before.

HERR OBER Jawohl, Herr Graf.

He bows again and goes off left. The COUNT *and* JEANNIE *smile at each other. A short pause.*

JEANNIE *(looks out left to the audience)* There's Stanley Smith again with yon Blonde. You'd think a man of his age would know better.

COUNT How shall he know? What is he? A provincial. She is his idea of the gay life. But let us speak of something more interesting. *(He puts out his cigarette)*

JEANNIE Did you hear them playing me in?

COUNT I beg your pardon?

JEANNIE The band. It was playing something else. When they saw me they merged into *(she says the name of the Scottish air)* "You'll tak' the High Road."

COUNT *(takes her hand—kisses it)* Already you are a favourite with everybody.

JEANNIE They're all so nice to me.

COUNT It cannot be otherwise. *(He looks at her with flattering admiration)* This gown...this gown. I like it so much. It becomes you the best.

JEANNIE You said the same about the other one.

COUNT Ah, yes, the little black one. But this has a special charm... It belongs to our first evening together. Do you remember it?

JEANNIE I'll never forget it as long as I live. To be with you at the Opera. I never thought music could sound like that. Not a bit like as if it was played by the human hand. Then when it was done and I thought it was time to go home to my bed, to come here instead. The soft lights and more music and champagne. It was like a fairy-tale come true. If I never get anything else out of life I can say I've lived. That's what everyone needs—to be able to say they've lived.

COUNT Why that they "have lived"? Why not that they "live"?

JEANNIE *(wistfully)* That's asking too much.

COUNT But why? *(He takes her hand. A short silence. He kisses her hand)* Has it been a happy day for you to-day?

JEANNIE Perfect. That motor ride into the country. The mountains with snow on the top and green grass below. And that lovely castle that used to belong to you. How can you bear to look at it after its being in your family all those hundreds of years?

COUNT Because soon, perhaps, it shall be in my family again.

JEANNIE *(immediately thrilled and interested)* Oh, how could that come to pass?

COUNT One hopes, madame; one hopes.

JEANNIE *(with a little sigh)* Hope's all that is left to us sometimes.

COUNT Do not speak so sad. To-night we must be gay. It is for us—how do you say—an anniversary.

JEANNIE An anniversary? What of?

COUNT Our first gala together.

JEANNIE We don't hold anniversaries each week. Only each year.

COUNT Do let us keep ours every week, eh?

JEANNIE I don't see how we can.

COUNT And why not?

JEANNIE I'll not be here. *(A pause; she makes up her mind),* Count, I've got something to say to you.

COUNT I listen. *(He smiles)* With two ears.

JEANNIE P'raps we'd wait till we've had our supper.

COUNT N-no. Do not keep me in suspense.

JEANNIE Uch, I'd rather. I meant to wait, anyhow.

COUNT I cannot wait. What wish you for to say me?

JEANNIE Only that to-morrow I've got to go home.

COUNT *(completely taken aback)* To-morrow? But no, madame!

JEANNIE I must.

COUNT Someone is ill?

JEANNIE No.

COUNT Did you receive a telegram? *(She shakes her head)* Then why must you go home?

JEANNIE Don't ask me.

COUNT But, madame? You say me you stay here one month. Now, after only one week, you go? Why?

JEANNIE I can't tell you. *(She turns away)*

COUNT After our so happy days together?

JEANNIE *(wistfully)* Have they been happy for you too?

COUNT *(takes her hand and kisses it)* More happy than for many, many years.

JEANNIE They've been the happiest of my whole life. I didn't know I could be so happy. I thought I'd missed it.

COUNT Then do not go away. Stay here, in Wien—in Vienna— with me.

JEANNIE How do you mean? With you?

COUNT Become my wife.

JEANNIE *(can't believe her ears)* Your wife? *(She removes her hand from his)*

COUNT *(with feeling)* How can I let you from my life now that I experience the joy of your company? I, who have gone through so much, know again the spring of love in my heart. You do this for me. Is it too much to hope that I do this also for you? Darling, say "I love you."

JEANNIE *(misty-eyed)* I like you very much.

COUNT Like? In English? That is not to love.

JEANNIE I'm Scotch—

COUNT *(tenderly)* So, you do love me?

JEANNIE Yes, I do. *(With a little breathless laugh)* Silly, isn't it?

COUNT Silly? How can you say such a thing! To love! The most beautiful—the most wonderful—the most noble—

STANLEY SMITH *enters by the door right.*

STANLEY Good evening, Miss McLean.

JEANNIE *(startled out of her mood)* It's you, is it?

The COUNT *rises and bows—moves slightly left and above his chair.*

STANLEY *(to the* COUNT*)* Don't get up, please.

COUNT I beg your pardon?

STANLEY Have it your way. *(To* JEANNIE*)* I've just come to remind you to-morrow's the last day of the Fair.

JEANNIE *(coldly)* What about it?

STANLEY I thought you wanted to have a look at my washing-machine.

JEANNIE I did. I don't now.

STANLEY Why not?

JEANNIE You know quite well.

STANLEY No, I don't. *(He refuses to be snubbed)* Go on. Tell me.

JEANNIE I'd rather not, in front of a third party.

STANLEY If I don't mind, why should you?

JEANNIE I told you I was a stickler for truth. Is that good enough for you?

STANLEY Not quite.

JEANNIE If you must have it in black and white! You made an engagement with me. I was quite willing to let you off for business—not for a blonde. That's a slight I can't forgive. Nor forget.

STANLEY I see.

JEANNIE As you're here you can be the first to congratulate me.

STANLEY Congratulate you? What on?

JEANNIE The Count and I are engaged— *(With a queenly gesture she gives her right hand to the* COUNT. *As* STANLEY *stares in astonishment)* —to be married.

STANLEY Married? *(A pause. He looks sharply from* JEANNIE *to the* COUNT, *and back to* JEANNIE *again)* Hur!

JEANNIE You're very rude.

STANLEY I mean to be. *(He turns on his heels and goes off down right)*

There is quite a long pause. The COUNT *seats himself.*

JEANNIE *(when she can control her fury)* Such cheek!

COUNT I congratulate madame. Among her many attributes she has dignity. Already I see her the so gracious chatelaine of the castle which has been in my family for so many hundreds of years.

JEANNIE *(awed)* You mean the one we saw to-day?

COUNT The one we have seen to-day. When...how soon...shall this be?

JEANNIE We'll need to wait a wee while.

COUNT But what for?

JEANNIE For your rents to come from your estates.

COUNT *(taken aback—pained)* You do not trust me?

JEANNIE Of course I trust you. But we'll need something to live on.

COUNT If you trust me, may we not continue to live on your fortune?

JEANNIE My fortune's done.

COUNT I beg your pardon?

JEANNIE My money's finished.

COUNT But you told me your father had died and left you his
fortune.

JEANNIE So he did. Two hundred pounds. I thought it would
last for ever. But it's gone. After paying for my clothes and
my room at the hotel and the extra meals and the trips
we've had, I've just about enough over to get home. *(She
half rises)* Why, what's the matter, are you not well?

The COUNT, *about to faint, has turned away and is
mopping his forehead.*

(really alarmed) Will I call the waiter to bring you some
brandy?

COUNT *(kisses her hand and pats it gently but with finality)*
No brandy, thank you—no brandy.

Curtain.

ACT III

Scene One

Three weeks later.

SCENE—The kitchen of an old-fashioned flat in Glasgow. The structure and the furniture are ugliest Victorian. Everything is polished to a turn. There is a cupboard bed up left covered by a curtain.

When the curtain has been up a moment we become aware of a pair of trousered legs right and, above them, an open newspaper. Below the legs are a pair of feet covered with thick hand-knitted woollen socks. During this scene we neither see the face nor hear the voice of the owner. A middle-aged WOMAN comes in. She should have a thin nose, the upper part of the bridge indented by the constant use of pince-nez, the chain of which is attached to her blouse by a round flat black knob.

MISTRESS *(as she comes in up left)* Where's that letter? *(She goes to an ornament on the mantelpiece, having to step over her husband's outstretched legs, takes out a cheap white envelope)* I'm sure she said seven. *(She takes a letter from the envelope and looks at her husband's feet as she does so)* There you are again without your slippers, Jevon! If I've told you once I've told you a hundred times I'll not have you ben the house without your slippers. You might be deaf and dumb for all the notice you take. Where are they...?

The feet do contortions under the chair and emerge wearing slippers. The MISTRESS crosses centre, unfolds

the letter and reads. When the husband has put on his
slippers he again stretches out his legs.

"Dear Madam, In reply to yours of to-day I'll be to see you
to-morrow at seven, Yours truly, Jeannie McLean." Just as I
thought. She's late. A bad start. If a servant can't be in time
for her first interview, when can she be in time? *(She folds
the letter, then sees something written on the back)* What's
this? "PS.—I stipulate no washing. Specially sheets." What
next! *(She puts the letter into the envelope and drops it on
the table left, then sits above the table and begins making
a paper firelighter, there being two or three finished ones
already on the table)* As I said to Mistress Drysdale this
afternoon when I was in buying the wool for your new socks:
"'Pon my word, Mistress Drysdale," I said, "I don't know
what on earth servants are coming to. Six in six months and
each one worse than the last. As for that last applicant," I
said, "I'll never forget the shock I had when I opened the
door to her. There she stood dressed for all the world like
a lady. I took one look at her. "What have you come for?" I
said. "The situation," she said. "Do you mean as a servant?"
I said. "I prefer to call it a housekeeper," she said. "You can
call it what you like," I said, "but not here," I said. And
I slammed the door in her face. You should have heard
Mistress Drysdale laugh. She fair split her sides. *(As the
old-fashioned door-bell clangs loudly)* That'll be her. What
does she think she's doing with the bell!

*She smoothes her hair unnecessarily, goes out, crosses
the hall, opens the door and speaks off.*

JEANNIE *(off diffidently)* Does Mistress Murdoch live here?

MISTRESS Aye.

JEANNIE Could I get speaking to her, please?

MISTRESS Is it Jeannie McLean?

JEANNIE Aye.

MISTRESS Go awa ben.

JEANNIE does so, to left centre MISTRESS *comes in again, followed by* JEANNIE, *who wears mackintosh and hat. She carries her handbag, and the umbrella at which the* MISTRESS *glances with disapproval.*

Could you not of left your umbrella in the stand?

JEANNIE Where is it?

The HUSBAND *drops the left slipper from his foot.*

MISTRESS Where it should be. Just inside the front door.

JEANNIE I couldn't see it. It was so dark.

MISTRESS It's no darker than most lobbies. Here. Give it to me. *(She takes the umbrella and goes out with it)*

The feet move. JEANNIE *glances at them. She gives a little start and seems uncertain whether to greet them or not. The* MISTRESS *comes in again.* JEANNIE *looks away from the feet guiltily, but not before the* MISTRESS *has seen her. She continues without lowering her voice.*

Yon's my husband. He doesn't like to be disturbed whilst he's reading "The Citizen." You're late. *(She sits in the chair left of the table)*

JEANNIE I know. I'm sorry. The car put me down the other end of the street.

MISTRESS Did you not tell the conductor the number?

JEANNIE He said it would be another haep'ny. I didn't see the sense, paying another haep'ny just to go the length of the street. It stretched longer than I thought.

MISTRESS Before we go any further, are you Orthodox?

JEANNIE *(shocked)* Of course.

MISTRESS What denomination?

JEANNIE U.P. *(A slight move nearer the table)*

MISTRESS That's all right. My last girl was a Catholic. She had always to be away to what she called "Mass" just when I needed her most. You'd not need to go to kirk except on your Sunday nights out?

JEANNIE That's so.

MISTRESS Mind you, I expect my girls to go to kirk and not to the cinema. We attend Byers Road. What previous experience have you had?

JEANNIE I kept house for my father.

MISTRESS Have you not been in service before?

JEANNIE No.

MISTRESS What about your reference?

JEANNIE I havena got one.

MISTRESS Do you expect to get a situation without a reference?

JEANNIE I'll just need to.

MISTRESS Have you a recommendation from your Minister?

JEANNIE No.

MISTRESS Could you get one?

JEANNIE No.

MISTRESS Why not?

JEANNIE I don't want him to know I'm back.

MISTRESS Back from where?

JEANNIE My holiday.

MISTRESS What holiday?

JEANNIE When my father died I went on a holiday.

MISTRESS Why do you not want your Minister to know you're back?

JEANNIE He's such an awful blether. Before you could say Jack Robinson it'd be all round the town.

MISTRESS Surely that's not the way to speak about a Minister.

JEANNIE It's the way to speak about ours.

MISTRESS *(obliged to let this pass)* Why do you not want it to get round the town?

JEANNIE I have my own reasons.

MISTRESS You'll require to tell me then.

JEANNIE I can't.

MISTRESS *(pause)* How am I to know you're respectable?

JEANNIE By my looks.

MISTRESS You can't go by looks.

JEANNIE Then in that case, Mistress Murdoch, I'll just wish you good evening. I'm sorry to have wasted your time. *(She turns up stage towards the door)*

MISTRESS Wait a minute. Not so fast. Perhaps we can come to an agreement. Who are you staying with the now?

JEANNIE *(slowly turning back)* I'm in lodgings.

MISTRESS How long have you been in them?

JEANNIE Three weeks.

MISTRESS Have you no relations in Glasgow?

JEANNIE Aye, I've two married cousins.

MISTRESS May I ask why you're not staying with them?

JEANNIE Aye. You may ask. *(Silence)*

MISTRESS *(obliged to let that pass too)* What wages do you want?

JEANNIE A pound a week.

The HUSBAND *drops a second slipper with a slight noise.*

MISTRESS A pound a week! Jevon, put your slippers on! Mercy on us! What do you think my husband's made of?

The feet move uncomfortably. JEANNIE *glances at them irresistibly, then quickly away again.*

JEANNIE What do you usually give?

MISTRESS Ten shillings. As you haven't a reference you'll be lucky to get that. Are you a good cook?

JEANNIE Aye.

MISTRESS Who's put you to the test?

JEANNIE Father.

MISTRESS You canna go by a member of your own family.

JEANNIE You could go by him. He was a rare grumbler, but he never left a lick on his plate.

MISTRESS What about your suet puddings?

JEANNIE *(up in arms)* What about them?

MISTRESS I never had a girl yet that could make a decent one.

JEANNIE I've still to come across the body that could say a word against mine. *(A slight move nearer the table)*

MISTRESS You'll need to do the stair and the close.

JEANNIE The stair! Do you mean the one I come up just now? The stone one?

MISTRESS Aye. We take it turn about with next door. Are you a good washer?

JEANNIE Aye. But as I stipulated in my letter, I don't want to do it.

MISTRESS Who do you think's going to do it, if not you?

JEANNIE Do you not send it out to the laundry?

MISTRESS The laundry? What next! I never sent a thing to the laundry in my life.

JEANNIE Do you not get in a washerwoman?

MISTRESS Not when I pay a servant.

JEANNIE *(after a pause)* What outings do you give?

MISTRESS Every other Sabbath after tea and an evening every other week.

JEANNIE Every other week?

MISTRESS *(firmly)* Aye.

JEANNIE And a whole day a month?

MISTRESS Half a day. After you've washed up the dinner dishes.

JEANNIE *(after a silence)* If I can start to-night, I'll accept.

MISTRESS *(suspiciously)* Why are you in such a hurry?

JEANNIE I don't want to break into another week's lodgings.

MISTRESS *(after a silence—an anxious one for JEANNIE)* I'll give you a month's trial. *(She rises)* You'll need to sleep in the cupboard-bed. *(She crosses up and indicates the bed. JEANNIE follows up to right of the MISTRESS)* I haven't a spare room. *(As they prepare to go)* I don't permit any smoking.

JEANNIE That's all right so far as I'm concerned. I don't know how.

MISTRESS And no followers allowed inside the front door.

JEANNIE *(with dignity)* Mistress Murdoch, you can make your mind quite easy on that score. I don't allow followers neither...inside nor out. Will that be all?

MISTRESS *(as they go)* For the noo!

They go.

Curtain.

Scene Two

SCENE—Three weeks later. The kitchen of the same flat. It looks fairly tidy, except for undried cups and saucers and saucepan on the drying-board. JEANNIE has been disturbed in the middle of washing-up. The pulley—a contraption that lets down from the ceiling—is filled with newly-washed, but not yet ironed, clothes.

As the curtain rises, we hear the MISTRESS's voice.

MISTRESS *(offstage)* Jeannie! *(Silence)*

Enter the MISTRESS left, wearing outdoor clothes.

Jeannie! Where's that girl? *(She sees the kitchen is empty, crosses right centre. Sees cups and saucers on board, goes to it. Exclaims)* The dinner dishes? Not done yet! Jeannie!

JEANNIE, carrying a too heavy clothes-basket, comes in left with difficulty. The MISTRESS hears her. Turns.

JEANNIE Aye. *(Entering)*

MISTRESS What's the meaning of this, Jeannie? *(She crosses up to right of the wheel-back chair)*

JEANNIE wears a blue overall. Her hair, which retains its "perm,'" is tousled by the wind.

JEANNIE *(breathlessly)* The meaning of what, ma'am? *(She plumps the basket on the floor in front of the table, with relief)*

MISTRESS Your washing-up not done at this time of day?

JEANNIE It came on to rain. I had to rescue my sheets.

MISTRESS You could have left them out. Rain's good for them.

JEANNIE *(to the pulley)* They might of got blown down. I didn't want to have to do them all over again.

MISTRESS *(to above the table)* Your dinner things should of been done long ago.

JEANNIE I was too busy.

MISTRESS What at?

JEANNIE My work. *(She lets down the pulley and begins to feel and turn the half-dry clothes)*

MISTRESS Judging by your sink, your work's still to do.

JEANNIE *(up in arms, turning to face the MISTRESS)* Mistress Murdoch, I don't like being behind with my work any more than you, but I've only got one pair of hands. How do you expect me to do a week's wash and cook a hot dinner as well? Aye, and a hot breakfast, too. I've been at it since six. *(She moves the stool from right of the stove, resets it in front of the wheel-back chair)*

MISTRESS The trouble with you, Jeannie, is you've no organization.

JEANNIE *(standing on the stool)* You canna organize acts of God.

MISTRESS That's profanity.

JEANNIE It's the truth. Are you away out? *(Removing the grey jumper—chemise—blue petticoat)*

MISTRESS Aye.

JEANNIE Before you go, have you time to take the other end of the sheets?

MISTRESS Can you not do them yourself?

JEANNIE No. They're that big. I get them all crooked.

MISTRESS I haven't time the now. I'm due at a meeting of the Girls' Friendly. You'll just need to wait till I get back.

JEANNIE *(still turning the clothes on the pulley)* Will you be in to his tea?

MISTRESS No. I'm glad you reminded me. *(She puts her handbag on the table and crosses to the dresser)* Here's his kipper. *(She unwraps the parcel on the dresser containing a kipper)*

JEANNIE *crosses to the table and rolls garments for ironing. The* **MISTRESS** *brings out a tea-caddy from the dresser cupboard and measures one-and-a-half teaspoonfuls of tea into a fairly large brown teapot and locks the cupboard and removes the key.*

And there's his tea. You can wait and take a cup out of his. What did you do with yon scon?

JEANNIE I ett it.

MISTRESS Ett it?

JEANNIE It was stale.

MISTRESS *(crossing to the stove, she places the teapot on it)* I was going to tell you to toast it for his tea. Did you not have enough for dinner?

JEANNIE No.

MISTRESS Why not? I gave you a good helping.

JEANNIE I told you before, Mistress Murdoch, I can't digest fat.

MISTRESS You could digest it quite well if you tried. For a girl in your position you're far too pernickety. The roast was underdone again to-day.

JEANNIE *(kneeling at the basket, worried)* I know. It's yon oven.

MISTRESS What's wrong with yon oven?

JEANNIE I can't get accustomed to it.

MISTRESS There's a lot of things you can't get accustomed to. Before you're fit for a gentleman's house you've a long way to go. Did you clean out your flue?

JEANNIE Aye. It's the coals.

MISTRESS What's wrong with the coals?

JEANNIE They're nothing but dross.

MISTRESS Do you expect me to supply you with the best "Brights" for the kitchen?

JEANNIE If we go on using dross we'll require to get the lum swept. It's started to smoke.

MISTRESS The lum was swept just before you came. *(She crosses to the table, picks up her handbag and gloves, and puts the key in her bag)* Mind you're dressed before he gets in. Good afternoon.

The MISTRESS *goes left.* JEANNIE *waits for the sound of the front door to close, then rises, crosses to the stove and slightly moves the kettle, then crosses to the cupboard-bed up left. From under the pillow she takes a packet of cigarettes and matches, crosses to the stool right centre, sits, takes out a cigarette and lights it— choking slightly—then puffs out the smoke, enjoying it more, when the bell goes. She gives a start—looks at her cigarette, rises, goes to the stove, where she puts the cigarette, still alight. The bell clangs again. She crosses to the cupboard-bed, hides the cigarettes and matches under the pillow, then goes out, muttering...*

Wait a minute! Wait a minute!

We hear the sound of her footsteps, then the door opening, then a familiar male voice.

STANLEY *(offstage)* Hello!

JEANNIE Mister Smith!

STANLEY *(offstage)* Aren't you going to ask me in?

JEANNIE I can't.

STANLEY Can't you, though? We'll see to that.

The door bangs. Footsteps. STANLEY SMITH *comes quickly into the kitchen.*

JEANNIE *(follows him in anxiously)* I told you I can't ask you in.

STANLEY *(to down centre)* That's why I came without being asked. *(He sees the pulley—amused)* Oh, washing! I've come on the right day seemingly.

JEANNIE *hastily takes down a pair of pants, a pair of stockings and a pair of socks.*

Don't bother to take it down for me. It makes me feel quite at home. *(A short pause)* Why couldn't you ask me in? What are you afraid of?

JEANNIE *(throws the washing into basket, but keeps the socks)* You'll get me into trouble. It's not my own house. *(She crosses below the table to left downstage end)*

STANLEY *(slight move up stage centre)* I know that. It belongs to some people called Murdoch. You're their "housekeeper," aren't you?

JEANNIE *(relentlessly begins business of turning and rolling socks)* No, I'm not. I'm their servant.

STANLEY Well?

JEANNIE Well, what?

STANLEY Is it as much like Paradise as you thought?

JEANNIE *(afraid of breaking down)* Will you please go?

STANLEY Not till you've answered my question. Is it as much like Paradise as you thought?

JEANNIE *(tries to sound convincing but on the verge of tears)* I like it fine.

STANLEY Do you? Then why are you looking so miserable? If I had a lass I'd be glad for her to be a servant, provided she found a good home. It's a more natural job for a girl than a shop or an office. *(Glancing round the kitchen)* Couldn't you have found something better than this?

JEANNIE No. I hadn't a reference. I had to take what I could get.

STANLEY You don't need a reference. They'd only to look at you.

JEANNIE That's what I thought. I was wrong. I answered advertisements till I was sick. When I applied here I was at my wits' end. And now that you've wormed it all out of me, would you please go? I want to be by myself.

STANLEY Why did you run away from Vienna?

JEANNIE You know quite well without asking. *(She puts the socks in the dresser drawer)*

STANLEY He thought you were a rich woman. You had to tell him you weren't. Was that it?

JEANNIE *(crosses below the table to the pulley and pulls up the line)* And what if it was? Have you come here to taunt me?

STANLEY Why didn't you let anyone know where you were?

JEANNIE Who, for instance?

STANLEY Your neighbour, Mrs. Whitelaw, for instance.

JEANNIE *(startled)* Mrs. Whitelaw! Have you been into communication with Mistress Whitelaw? *(Up to STANLEY)*

STANLEY More than communication. I've seen her.

JEANNIE *(fears the worst)* Seen her? Have you given me away?

STANLEY No. Surely you know me better than that?

JEANNIE Who else have you seen?

STANLEY Your cousins.

JEANNIE My cousins? Here in Glasgow? You shouldn't have done that.

STANLEY Why not?

JEANNIE I don't want them here. A place like this. I wish you'd go. He'll be in for his tea. *(Over to the sink—dries cups and saucers)*

STANLEY Who's "he"?

JEANNIE Her husband.

STANLEY If he's anything like "her," I don't wonder you're afraid.

JEANNIE He's a very kind wee man. What do you know about "her," anyway?

STANLEY I think I passed her just now, on the stairs.

JEANNIE The now? Did she see you stop at the door?

STANLEY Would it matter very much if she had?

JEANNIE Aye, would it! I'm not allowed followers. *(Corrects herself hastily)* I mean gentlemen.

STANLEY Thanks for the compliment. Don't be alarmed. She didn't see me. I'm not such a fool as I look.

JEANNIE I'm glad of that. *(She crosses and hangs the cups and stands the saucers on the dresser)*

STANLEY You can still hold your own, I see.

JEANNIE Aye, and I hope I'll always be able to.

STANLEY Then what are you afraid of?

JEANNIE Don't keep all on using that word. I'm not afraid.

STANLEY Then why all this secrecy?

JEANNIE Uch. *(She crosses to the sink—picks up and dries the saucepan)* I don't want everyone to know what a sapsy I've been—spending all my money so quick and having to come back from my holiday so soon.

STANLEY *(very much the Yorkshire business-man)* You don't mean to tell me you've spent all that money in a week?

JEANNIE *(wishes she hadn't given herself away—defiant)* Aye.

STANLEY Two hundred pounds?

JEANNIE Aye. *(She thinks she might as well be killed for a sheep as a lamb)* Not counting the journey. I didna let on at the time, but I had a bit over for that—enough to cover my meals in the train—*and* my share of the tips.

STANLEY You're a bigger fool than I thought.

JEANNIE You don't require to rub it in.

STANLEY How much did you give him?

JEANNIE Who? *(She puts the saucepan on the shelf)*

STANLEY The Count. How much did you give him in hard cash?

JEANNIE I didn't give him anything.

STANLEY Rubbish. Come on, out with it. How much?

JEANNIE Mr. Smith *(slight move centre, dish-cloth in hand)*, you're being very impertinent. If I liked to pay for our outings that's no business of yours.

STANLEY Did you pay for them yourself, or hand him over the money to do it for you?

JEANNIE I handed it over, of course.

STANLEY I thought as much. Did you count the change?

JEANNIE No, I didn't. I've more manners when I'm with a gentleman.

STANLEY You were fairly careful when you were settling up with me.

JEANNIE I said a "gentleman."

STANLEY That's what you called me a while back.

JEANNIE It was a slip of the tongue. *(To the sink—hangs up the glass cloth)*

STANLEY *(nettled)* Gentleman or no gentleman, he must have made a damn good thing out of you. You can't say I didn't warn you.

JEANNIE *(up to STANLEY)* And who were you to warn me? Whose fault was it I went out with him in the first place?

STANLEY You can't blame me for your own stupidity.

JEANNIE I do blame you. Anyone'd be stupid after having their hopes raised and then getting a disappointment like yon.

STANLEY You mean when I let you down about going round the town that night?

JEANNIE Aye, but you'd perfect right to please yourself. I'm sorry I referred to it.

STANLEY I shouldn't have done it, I admit, but that doesn't excuse you for being such a little fool.

JEANNIE Mr. Smith, would you please to mind your own business? Go on away from here. Go on. Get out. If you come again I'll slam the door in your face.

STANLEY I've taken the hell of a lot of trouble to find you, you know.

JEANNIE That's your own look-out. And I'll thank you not to swear at me. I don't permit it.

STANLEY You're enough to make any man swear.

JEANNIE *(pause)* If you won't go I'll just need to ignore you and get on with my work. *(She goes to the clothes-basket and takes out a large double-bedded sheet)*

STANLEY *crosses up to the door—turns and sees* JEANNIE. *After watching her struggles for a moment he takes off his coat and hangs it and his hat on a peg above the door.*

STANLEY Here, you can't manage those sheets by yourself.

JEANNIE I can manage quite well, thank you.

STANLEY No, you can't. *(He takes the other end of the sheet, moves right and helps methodically. He knows all the right moves)* When I was a kid I used to give my mother a hand with the folding.

They get on with it.

She gave me hot dripping toast for being a good lad. *(The final fold brings them together)* Have I been a good lad?

JEANNIE *takes the sheet and turns away to hide her tears. Moving up stage left to top end of the table.*

Nay, lass, don't cry.

JEANNIE I don't know what on earth I'm crying for. *(Folding a sheet)*

STANLEY I do. You're crying because you expected life to be like Paradise, and it's not.

A short pause. She tries to stem her tears.

This place has got you down. Come on out of it!

JEANNIE *(helplessly)* Where'll I go?

STANLEY Come with me.

JEANNIE *(turns to him. Immediately up in arms)* Mister Smith, what are you suggesting?

STANLEY I'm suggesting that you should marry me.

JEANNIE Marry you? What for?

STANLEY For fun!

JEANNIE Is this a joke?

STANLEY No.

JEANNIE You mean you'd marry me when I was down and out—like this?

STANLEY What difference does that make?

JEANNIE It makes a lot of difference to me. I thank you very much. I'm very grateful to you. *(She puts a sheet on the upstage end of the table)*

STANLEY Don't put it like that, please.

JEANNIE *(to the front edge of the table)* But I am. You've given me back my self-respect. That's a very big thing.

STANLEY Had you lost it?

JEANNIE Of course. You're bound to lose your self-respect when you think someone's wanted you for yourself, and then you find out it's for your money—spec'lly when your money's all gone.

STANLEY That's a bit of a pill, isn't it? *(Silence)* Well? What's your answer?

JEANNIE My answer's "No."

STANLEY Why?

JEANNIE If you think I'm the sort to take advantage of your kindness, you don't know me.

STANLEY Kindness?

JEANNIE What else is it? Why else would you ask me?

STANLEY I told you. For fun. You make me laugh.

JEANNIE That's easy. Men like you laugh at anything. I'm no use to you. I'm a failure. The Mistress says I don't even know how to cook. It's yon oven.

STANLEY I'm inventing a fool-proof oven. *(He crosses to the open oven)*

JEANNIE Are you? That should be a success. How did you get on with your washing-machine?

STANLEY It was a failure, too.

JEANNIE Was it? I'm awful sorry. How was that?

STANLEY *(down right)* You didn't come to look at it.

JEANNIE No, but honestly?

STANLEY I was up against competition.

JEANNIE Like the rest of us. How's yon blonde?

STANLEY I don't know.

JEANNIE I thought you were in love with her.

STANLEY. Come to that, I thought you were in love with the Count? What back answer have you got to that?

JEANNIE Just that I *was* in love with him.

STANLEY Come to that, I was in love with the Blonde. It took me exactly a week to get over it—just as it took you exactly a week to get over the Count.

JEANNIE It didn't. I'm not over him. I'm in love with him still. *(She sprinkles the clothes angrily. Sprinkling another rough-dried garment and rolling it up)* That's why I don't care how hard I work. It tires you out. You can't think so hard when you're tired out. *(She hears the noise of the kettle)* What's that? *(She turns—sees it)* Oh, my—my grate! *(She runs to it)*

STANLEY What's the matter?

JEANNIE *(lifts it off the fire and replaces it on the hob)* The kettle's boiled over on to my clean grate.

STANLEY *(gets in the way)* Don't touch it. You'll burn yourself. Let me.

JEANNIE *(running round below* STANLEY *and up to the chest of drawers—takes a duster from the drawer)* You great big sapsy, did you not see it? *(She kneels to wipe the grate and hearth)*

STANLEY *(doesn't object to being bullied by her)* No.

JEANNIE And you staring at it all the time. *(Down above* STANLEY *to the grate)* Go on away. I've got to get my work done and my dress changed before he gets in.

STANLEY When's that?

JEANNIE Twenty-five past six.

STANLEY You've just time to give me a cup of tea before I go. You've got some boiling water. *(He sees it on the hob and also sees cigarette-end that* JEANNIE *has been smoking)* Does she smoke?

JEANNIE Who?

STANLEY The Mistress.

JEANNIE The Mistress? No.

STANLEY Who's been smoking in here, then?

JEANNIE I have.

STANLEY You? I thought you didn't know how.

JEANNIE I've learned.

STANLEY What made you do that?

JEANNIE It soothes my nerves.

STANLEY You? With nerves?

JEANNIE Why shouldn't I have them the same as other people? *(She throws the cloth in the pail)* Anyhow, what's it got to do with you?

STANLEY Where's the teapot? *(He finds it on the hob and looks inside)* She's been a bit skinny with the tea. Where's the caddy? *(To centre)*

JEANNIE She has it locked.

STANLEY Does she lock up everything?

JEANNIE Aye. I *told* you I hadn't a reference.

STANLEY Good God! *(He crosses to the stove above* **JEANNIE**, *lifts the kettle and pours the water into the teapot)*

JEANNIE *(in a panic)* But here, I'll lose my place.

STANLEY Don't worry about that. We'll leave it there to mash a bit. Where's the cosy?

He puts the teapot on the hob, goes to the stove, unhooks the cosy and throws it to **JEANNIE**, *who puts it mechanically on to the teapot.* **STANLEY** *crosses to the dresser, takes the tray from the side of the dresser.* **JEANNIE** *puts the teapot on the floor near her.*

Now the cups and saucers. *(He puts them on the tray)* Milk and sugar. *(He finds them)* She's been a bit skinny with the milk too. Get the buffet ready, lass. *(He moves the stool to centre, puts the tray on it, turns the armchair down stage near the stool and sits)* Now, lass, pour out. Don't look as if the end of the world had come.

JEANNIE *pours out and hands him a cup. He drinks and puts the cup down.*

Not so bad! *(He tales out a packet of cigarettes)* Have a cigarette?

JEANNIE No, thanks.

STANLEY *(puts one between her lips)* Come on, you know you like it.

JEANNIE *takes it from her lips while he lights a match. She obeys and puts it between her lips again; he holds the flame.*

Don't blow—puff.

JEANNIE I'm all right when I get started. *(She tastes the tea— with the spoon)*

STANLEY Do you remember the first meal we had together?

JEANNIE I'll never forget it.

STANLEY Neither will I.

JEANNIE It was the first time I tasted champagne.

STANLEY Is that the only reason?

JEANNIE No.

STANLEY What other?

JEANNIE It was the first time I ett a dinner I hadn't helped to cook.

STANLEY I hoped you were going to say "Because of the pleasant company."

JEANNIE As I remarked before, "Hope's all that's left to us sometimes."

STANLEY You didn't remark it to me.

JEANNIE Didn't I? It must have been to some other man.

STANLEY I believe you're a dark horse.

JEANNIE Maybe I am.

STANLEY At last?

JEANNIE "At last" what?

STANLEY A smile—a "wee" smile.

JEANNIE It's the tea and the cigarette. They go well together.

STANLEY Dope.

JEANNIE Uch, you need a bit of dope once in a while.

STANLEY Only if you're unhappy.

JEANNIE Who isn't? Who's happy?

STANLEY I could be.

JEANNIE So could I. But who is?

STANLEY The lucky ones that have the right companion to come back to after their day's work. *(A short silence)* Did you really mean—what you said about still being in love with the Count?

JEANNIE No—not really. It was only the way he kissed my hand. It seemed like romance. But what's the use of romance if there's no truth in it? I'm a stickler for truth. That's why I finished with you. Both of you deceived me. I'll never trust a man again so long as I live. I hate lies.

STANLEY Considering you're such a good little liar yourself!

JEANNIE Me? A liar? What do you mean?

STANLEY How old are you?

JEANNIE *(caught out)* Ooh! *(When she can speak)* A woman's allowed to take a slice off her age. It's understood.

STANLEY And it's understood that a man's allowed to say he's met a business friend—or words to that effect. What made you angry was not so much the lie as the fact that I wanted to go out with the Blonde instead of you. It was very silly of me—showed my bad taste. I'm sorry. I can promise you it won't happen again.

JEANNIE How did you know I told a lie about my age?

STANLEY I saw it in your passport.

JEANNIE You'd a cheek looking in my passport.

STANLEY How could I help myself when you showed me your photo?

JEANNIE That awful thing!

STANLEY Jeannie—

JEANNIE Who gave you leave to call me by my Christian name?

STANLEY Mine's "Stanley."

JEANNIE I know that—Mister Smith.

STANLEY Miss McLean—if you'll let me call you by your Christian name I'll throw in a washing-machine.

JEANNIE That's bribery and corruption.

STANLEY (takes her hand and kisses it with more sincerity than grace) I may not be able to kiss your hand as well as the Count—

JEANNIE (her eyes misty) You're doing fine.

STANLEY Will you marry me, Jeannie?

JEANNIE (moved) If you really mean what you said about the washing-machine.

STANLEY I'll throw in a fool-proof oven as well.

JEANNIE Then I've no alternative—Stanley.

STANLEY kisses her.

Curtain.

VISIT THE
SAMUEL FRENCH
BOOKSHOP
AT THE
ROYAL COURT THEATRE

Browse plays and theatre books, get expert advice and enjoy a coffee

Samuel French Bookshop
Royal Court Theatre
Sloane Square
London
SW1W 8AS
020 7565 5024

Shop from thousands of titles on our website

 samuelfrench.co.uk

 samuelfrenchltd

 samuel french uk

Lightning Source UK Ltd.
Milton Keynes UK
UKHW020959231118
332815UK00005B/180/P